Ripley's Believe It or Not!®

Vice President, Licensing & Publishing Amanda Joiner
Creative Content Manager Sabrina Sieck

Editor Jordie R. Orlando
Text Geoff Tibballs
Feature Contributors Engrid Barnett, Jordie R. Orlando
Fact-checker & Proofreader Rachel Paul
Indexer Yvette Chin
Special Thanks Steve Campbell, Yaneisy Contreras, John Corcoran, Steph Distasio, Julia Moellmann, Kurtis Moellmann, Colton Kruse, and Matt Mamula

Designer Luis Fuentes
Reprographics Bob Prohaska
Cover Artwork Luis Fuentes

ISBN 978-1-60991-480-6
ISBN 978-1-60991-497-4 [Walmart U.S.]
ISBN 978-1-60991-498-1 [Costco Canada]
ISBN 978-1-60991-499-8 [Indigo]

For more information regarding permission, contact:
Vice President, Licensing & Publishing
Ripley Entertainment Inc.
7576 Kingspointe Parkway, Suite 188
Orlando, Florida 32819
publishing@ripleys.com
www.ripleys.com/books

Manufactured in China in May 2021 by Leo Paper
First Printing

Library of Congress Control Number: 2021934183

PUBLISHER'S NOTE
While every effort has been made to verify the accuracy of the entries in this book, the Publisher cannot be held responsible for any errors contained in the work. They would be glad to receive any information from readers.

WARNING
Some of the stunts and activities are undertaken by experts and should not be attempted by anyone without adequate training and supervision.

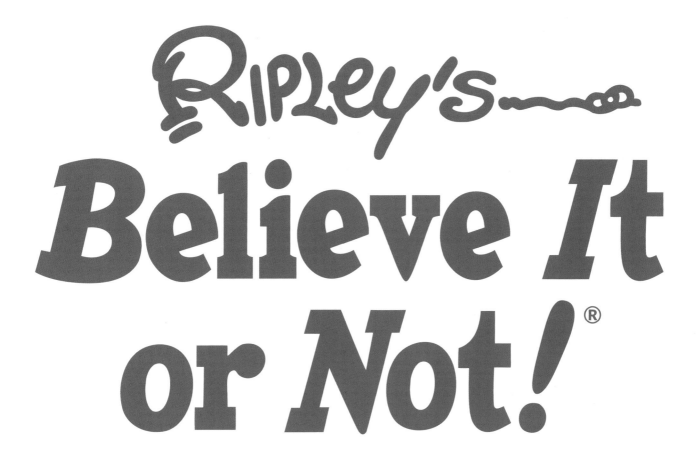

Ripley's
Believe It or Not!®

PUBLISHING

a Jim Pattison Company

UNBOXING WHAT'S INSIDE

45
HAIR-RAISING FEATS

57
STRANGE CREATIONS

120
ASTOUNDING ANIMALS

SPECIAL FEATURES:

Believe It or Not! BIO

Take a deep dive into the unbelievable lives of historical and contemporary figures.

...OR NOT!®

Learn the surprising truth behind common misconceptions.

223
BIZARRE TECHNOLOGY

149
NATURAL WONDERS

228
AMAZING CULTURES

Get a glimpse of the rare and
unusual exhibits found inside
the Ripley's Warehouse.

Check out the astounding
submissions from your
fellow Ripley's fans!

Get to know the people behind
the pictures in interviews you
won't find anywhere else!

FAIR PLAY

The very first Ripley's Believe It or Not! Odditorium was at the 1933 World's Fair in Chicago!

International expositions like the World's Fair give countries the opportunity to show off their latest cultural and industrial achievements. Robert Ripley, the founder of Ripley's Believe It or Not!, was one of the most popular people in the U.S. during the 1930s, and it only made sense to bring his wildly successful cartoon to life with a museum at the World's Fair.

The museum, an "Odditorium," saw an astounding two million visitors. Inside were dozens of Ripley's famous cartoons, live performers, and hundreds of strange and exotic artifacts Ripley acquired from his worldly travels. In fact, Ripley traveled so much that by this time he already had a catchy nickname—"The Modern Marco Polo." The success of the first Odditorium led to several more appearances at world expositions across the country.

To celebrate the earliest Odditoriums, a selection of vintage Ripley's Believe It or Not! poster designs were made available on our new online shop, **RipleysStore.com!**

WHAT'S NEW?

CAVILL AV

THE NEXT BIG THING

The Odditorium at Surfers Paradise, Queensland, Australia, has a new resident: Ring-O, the 29-ft-wide (9-m) blue-ringed octopus! Actual blue-ringed octopuses only grow to about 8 in (20 cm) long, yet they are one of the most venomous marine animals in the world. But Ring-O isn't the only thing to look out for in Surfers Paradise—the Odditorium was also updated with four new galleries and a state-of-the-art 7D Moving Theatre!

ADORABLE ADDITION

In March 2020, Ripley's Aquarium of Myrtle Beach in South Carolina welcomed a waddle of African penguins to their newly built Penguin Playhouse! About seven months later, Egerton arrived—the first penguin chick to hatch at the Aquarium! This was exciting not just because Egerton is adorable, but also because African penguins are one of the most endangered penguin species in the world. They are the only penguins found in Africa, preferring warmer water temperatures unlike their Antarctic counterparts.

HELLO
My name is
EGERTON

THE SCIENCE OF Ripley's Believe It or Not!®

PIC STOP!
SNAP & SHARE
#azboardwalk
#ripleysaz

WEIRD SCIENCE

Arizonans have been enjoying *The Science of Ripley's Believe It or Not!*, an interactive collaboration between Ripley's and the Science North museum. Since February 2021, guests have been able to learn not just what our exhibits are, but how and why they got that way. Some of the oddities included in the Scottsdale attraction are a life-size model of a prehistoric snake, micro-sculptures that fit within the eye of a needle, and a real two-headed cow!

NEW IN NEWPORT

After about a year of extensive renovations, Ripley's Believe It or Not! World of Adventure in Newport, Oregon, is once again open for fun! In addition to 11 themed galleries filled with more than 500 strange and unusual exhibits, visitors can also strike a pose next to their favorite celebrities and superheroes at Louis Tussaud's Waxworks. Outside of the building is an odd art garden, featuring a massive gorilla made from tires and a 3,500-lb (1,588-kg) redwood bench carved in the shape an octopus.

SOMETHING FOR EVERYONE

We're delivering the digital goods with five new online video series!

Each series is hosted by a member of the Ripley's crew who uses their expertise to bring you the most unbelievable stories, food, exhibits, facts, and more. With so many weird and wonderful topics, there's something for everyone to enjoy!

RIPLEY's REWIND

Hosted by social-savvy Steph Distasio, Ripley's Rewind highlights the strange in an age of boomers, millennials, and beyond! With throwbacks, pop culture, TV, and trends that totally swept the nation, we're talking everything from sea monkeys to Carmen Sandiego. This series takes it back to your favorite childhood moments and, of course, adds in a little Ripley's spin.

Believe It or Not!® BITES

What's cooking in the Ripley's kitchen? Video producer by day, chef by night, Matt Mamula is serving up the strange on Believe It or Not! Bites. Grab a glass of circus-born pink lemonade, paired with a 1,500-year-old Roman hamburger, and you've got yourself a meal (and a story for the dinner table).

After DARK

Stepping out of the ordinary and into the totally taboo, Ripley's After Dark brings the macabre and unexplained to the surface. Join our fearless host and creative content queen, Sabrina Sieck, as she uncovers the truth about Countess Elizabeth Báthory's blood baths, spills the tea on Lizzie Borden's alleged murder weapon, and examines the remains of the Vampire of Düsseldorf. All fact-based, all true, and all After Dark.

Ripley's HISTORY [OFF THE RECORD]

This isn't your average history lesson... or your average history teacher! Colton Kruse, curator of digital content and history buff extraordinaire, is eager to share some peculiar pages that you likely won't find in your textbook. What was the worst year in history? Who was the real Dr. Frankenstein? Dig a little deeper into these questions and more as we enter a strange past on Ripley's History Off the Record.

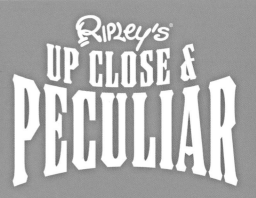

Ripley's UP CLOSE & PECULIAR

We're bringing the weird to a personal level with our exhibits buyer, Kurtis Moellmann! Up Close & Peculiar brings you straight to the shelves of the Ripley's Warehouse with pieces for every pop culture junkie and oddities collector alike. Follow along with Kurtis as he brings Ripley's-exclusive exhibits right out of our collection and onto your screen.

HOPE FLOATS

The city of New Orleans, Louisiana, refused to let a pandemic rain on their parade—specifically, their world-famous Mardi Gras celebrations!

In lieu of a traditional parade, thousands of homes in the area were transformed into "house floats," complete with over-the-top decorations that captured the spirit of Carnival season. Themes as diverse as dinosaurs and board games to Dolly Parton and crawfish boils lined the streets. People were encouraged to view the floats on their own time, safe from the risks of large gatherings. The creative solution also provided a way for local artists who had been hit hard by the pandemic to earn money.

EXPENSIVE STUDY

A steppe eagle named Min left Russian scientists with hundreds of dollars in roaming charges after it flew into Iranian territory. The bird had been fitted with a device to track its migration route from Siberia, but the charges skyrocketed when the eagle flew from Kazakhstan into Iran, where each message it sent cost around $1.

PET KEEPSAKE

Theresa Furrer, of Pittsburgh, Pennsylvania, spins the fur from dogs and cats into hats and scarves that can be worn by their grieving owners after their pet has passed. The process, called "catgora" (for cats) and "chiengora" (for dogs), involves spinning fur into a textile yarn. She had the idea for her Nine Lives Twine business following the death of her own pet cat, Cleo.

SOLITARY CAT

To avoid disturbing the ecological balance of the region, all cats are banned on the Norwegian archipelago of Svalbard, so the only feline on the islands—a ginger cat named Kesha—is officially registered as a fox!

ALLEY DOGS

Blake and Adam—two goldendoodle dogs owned by Terri Simpson—go bowling at their very own alley in Emmett, Idaho. By pushing the ball off a child's bowling ramp with their paws, the dogs have a high score of 109 and sometimes even get strikes and spares. Simpson has been training them to bowl since they were around 12 weeks old, and after successful bowls, they often high-five her.

> **Green herons frequently use bait to catch fish. They drop twigs, feathers, insects, and pieces of bread onto the water surface to lure fish within reach.**

POOP SUICIDE

The *Ananteris balzanii* scorpion from South America has its anus located at the end of its tail, right next to its stinger. If it loses its tail to a predator or chooses to amputate the tail to avoid capture, the scorpion can never defecate again and will likely die from accumulated waste that causes its body to balloon in size.

DEATH TRAP

Female *Photuris* fireflies mimic the flash patterns of other firefly species to lure unsuspecting males to their deaths. By preying on the males of other species, the *Photuris* female can acquire their toxins, which are then deposited into her eggs to act as a chemical defense.

BEAR FREED

Police officers in Placer County, California, helped free a huge black bear that was trapped inside a dumpster. The bear, known locally as T-shirt because the white patch of fur on his chest makes it look like he is wearing a T-shirt, had climbed in looking for something to eat.

ARACHNOBUTT

The spider-tailed horned viper of Iran is a venomous snake whose tail has a bulbous end bordered by long, drooping scales that make it look like a spider. The snake moves the tip of its tail back and forth across the ground to lure in spider-eating birds. The rest of the snake stays perfectly still until the bird is within striking range.

IT'S A TRAP!

FLIES DISGUISE

The *Macrocilix maia* moth of Southeast Asia has wing markings that look like flies eating bird poop!

The moth evolved this trait to deter predators, who instinctively avoid insects feasting on bird droppings, as they are more likely to carry diseases. It is not unusual for animals to use mimicry as a way to hide or frighten predators—there are praying mantises that look like flowers, caterpillars that pretend to be snakes, and butterflies with owl eye spots on their wings, for instance—but rarely do they recreate entire scenes. Believe it or not, the moth also gives off an odor that smells like bird poop!

COIN HAUL

In 2019, metal-detecting couple Adam Staples and Lisa Grace unearthed a haul of 1,000-year-old coins in a field in Somerset, England, that are worth up to $6.5 million. The 2,528 coins date back to the time of William the Conqueror and represent the largest Norman treasure find since 1833.

MISSING RING

In 1957 when he was 17, Roy Beddows lost a gold ring while working on a farm in Shropshire, England. The ring was found in the field 61 years later and, because it was engraved with his initials, was able to be returned to him.

BANK BILLS

Even though they are not for circulation and are kept safely locked away in a vault, the Bank of England regularly prints a small number of £100 million bills (worth $130 million), known as *titans*.

FOUR YOLKS

Diane Olver, from Merseyside, England, cracked open an egg and found that it contained four separate yolks, beating the odds of 11 billion to one.

PIZZA TIME

Chicago product designer Claire Hogan created a working clock out of a real pizza! She used 12 evenly-spaced pepperoni slices as a way to mark the numbers that would appear on a normal clock. After baking the pie, she let it cool and then smothered it in a clear resin to preserve its appearance (while also rendering it inedible, unfortunately). Once the resin dried, she added the clock mechanisms. Now it can be pizza time, any time!

FAN FEED

HEFTY HARVEST

Kendra Williams of Houston, Texas, accidentally grew a 20-lb (9-kg) sweet potato! She shared this photo with Ripley's and told us how she was digging up her second-ever harvest of sweet potatoes when she found this behemoth that had been left behind from the previous year's harvest. She named the potato "Patricia" and went on tour with the tuber, showing it off to friends, family, and even local news and radio stations! Patricia ended up being turned into sweet potato hash and pie filling. Williams told us "they were really good and tasted like a normal sweet potato."

BEDAZZLED

Everything in this kitchen is covered in beads!

Artist Liza Lou spent five years hand-gluing beads on everything in this full-scale, 168-sq-ft (15.6-sq-m) room. Many of the objects, like the curtains, are formed out of papier-mâché. The rest of the room is constructed from wood, plaster, and wire, except for the appliances, which the artist upcycled from her own kitchen. Lou says the work is a monument to unsung labor. The piece, titled *Kitchen*, is currently on display at the Whitney Museum of American Art in New York City.

Even the water in the sink is made of beads!

SnotBot®

Marine biologists use a drone called the SnotBot® to collect samples of water blasted from a whale's blowhole.

Drones are also able to capture high-quality photos, which are equally as helpful to scientists!

A whale's "blow," a term for the water they exhale, includes a wealth of information that scientists can use to determine the creature's health, stress levels, and more. The SnotBot® collects this data by flying through the whale's exhaled water condensate (a.k.a. snot or blow) with petri dishes. Scientists can then take those petri dishes to a lab and study them. Drones are much less intrusive than other means of data collection and are faster than boats—the SnotBot® can fly up to 50 mph (80.5 kmph)! For these reasons, drones have become an invaluable resource for studying marine creatures.

RIGHT ON TARGET!

Before drones, marine biologists would try to follow the whales in boats, which can't always keep up with the massive creatures.

Drones are noninvasive, meaning the data scientists retrieve from the snot is less likely to be altered by the stress a whale might experience by being around boats.

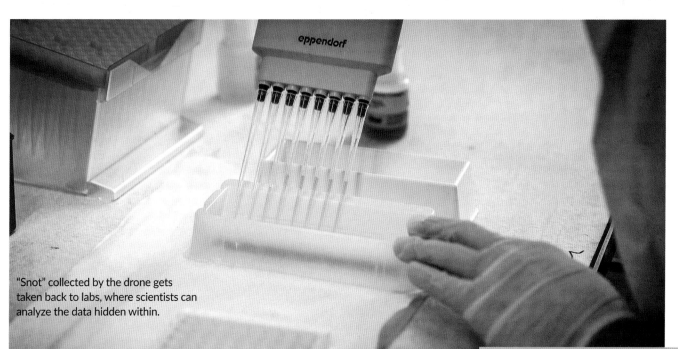

"Snot" collected by the drone gets taken back to labs, where scientists can analyze the data hidden within.

BUN IN A MILLION

Ran, a bread artist from Tokyo, bakes intricate designs into dough that are only revealed when the loaf has been sliced.

From a bagel hiding blue and red flowers to a detailed Rowlet caught inside a Poké Ball bun, Ran's remarkable bakes are the best thing since sliced—well, you know. Other culinary delights include edible reproductions of fine art like Leonardo da Vinci's *Mona Lisa*, Vermeer's *Girl with a Pearl Earring*, and Vincent Van Gogh's *Sunflowers*. Talk about appetizing artistry!

WROTE NAKED

French novelist Victor Hugo, author of *Les Misérables*, wrote naked to avoid procrastinating. His valet would take Hugo's clothes, lock him in a room, and return them only when he had finished writing for the day.

GERM ART

The American Society of Microbiology runs an annual competition for the best artwork made from live bacteria—a process called agar art, or germ art. Past entries have included a bacterial replica of Vincent van Gogh's *Starry Night*.

NAME CHANGE

U.S. actor Albert Brooks, who provided the voice of Nemo's father in *Finding Nemo*, was born Albert Einstein. He changed his name when he was in his teens.

TWAIN'S STRUGGLE

It took Mark Twain about eight years to write *The Adventures of Huckleberry Finn*—and it proved so difficult that he completed three other books in the meantime.

Elvis Presley Fight Scene

On this site, the corner of Hwy 51 and East Washington Avenue around 1 am, on June 24th, 1977, Elvis Presley was riding in the 2nd of two limousines which had stopped for a red light. He was coming from a concert in Des Moines and had just arrived in Madison. Elvis noticed a young teen on the ground being beaten by two other youths here at the former Skyland Service Station. Elvis jumped out of his limo and moved quickly to the fight scene. They admitted later that they knew it was the legendary Elvis Presley who was standing in front of them in his classic karate stance saying, "I'll take you on". After a few classic karate moves by Elvis, the youths recognized him, stood and shook hands and promised to stop fighting. Elvis asked "Is everything settled now"? Elvis was on his way to the Sheraton and his last Madison appearance. He died 52 days later, on August 16th, 1977.

KARATE KING

On the corner of Highway 51 and East Washington Avenue in Madison, Wisconsin, there is a stone plaque commemorating the time Elvis Presley allegedly broke up a fight using his martial arts skills. On June 24, 1977, Elvis's limousine was stopped at a red light when he noticed a street fight involving three youths. A black belt in karate, Presley jumped out of the car and intervened. When the combatants saw "the King" standing before them in a menacing karate pose, they immediately agreed to stop fighting and shook hands. Presley died 52 days later.

MARBLE PILLOWS
Norwegian sculptor Håkon Anton Fagerås creates realistic pillows from hard, white marble. He uses pneumatic drills and hammers to form the creases and folds necessary to make his artistic marble pillows look exactly like soft, feather-filled ones... but not as comfortable.

KLINGON THREATS
After actor Malcolm McDowell's character Tolian Soran caused the death of Captain Kirk in the 1994 movie *Star Trek Generations*, McDowell received a series of death threats, some of them written in Klingon!

TORTURE TRAINING
To help prepare for the daily 8.5 hours in makeup necessary for him to be transformed into the Grinch, Jim Carrey was trained by a CIA officer who specialized in teaching agents how to withstand torture. Carrey had to don the Grinch makeup for more than 100 days of filming.

Local artist Michael Long creates detailed miniature replicas of the dive bars of Santa Barbara, California, complete with tiny bar stools, beer taps, and wine bottles.

NO MUSTACHES
Actor David Cross had to fight the FOX network to keep Tobias Fünke's mustache on *Arrested Development*, as at the time FOX executive Gail Berman had a "no mustaches" policy for comedy shows.

DISTANT COUSINS
While filming the 2019 movie *A Beautiful Day in the Neighborhood*, Tom Hanks discovered that he is related to children's TV host Fred Rogers, whom he plays in the film. The pair are sixth cousins.

TYPEWRITER ORCHESTRA
Members of the Boston Typewriter Orchestra, founded in 2004, use old typewriters to produce music.

NEWSPAPER MODELS
Japanese artist Atsushi Adachi makes amazingly detailed models of historical battleships and combat planes out of old newspapers from the same period. He has also made a miniature version of Neil Armstrong's space suit from old newspaper clippings.

50 STATES

By completing a race in Des Moines, Iowa, on October 20, 2019, Aiden Jaquez, of Montgomery, Illinois, had run half-marathons in all 50 states by the age of 11. He ran his first half-marathon at age six in Sarasota, Florida.

SKATEBOARD RIDE

Australians Dwayne Kelly and Dan Roduner rode 644 mi (1,036 km) across Texas on electric skateboards. The trip took them 12 days, and they survived two tornados en route.

WINDSURFING GRANNY

Eighty-one-year-old grandmother Anastasia Gerolymatou, from Kefalonia, Greece, windsurfed 18 mi (29 km) across the Ionian Sea in six hours from Kefalonia to Kyllini. She has been windsurfing for more than 40 years.

NOVEL SKILL

Fourteen-year-old Monty Lord, from Bolton, England, can identify 129 books—including William Shakespeare's plays, Ian Fleming's James Bond books, and J. K. Rowling's Harry Potter books—just by hearing their first sentence.

STATIONARY BIKE

Ben Miles, the owner of a restaurant in Mallorca, Spain, rode a stationary bike for 277 hours straight—that's more than 11 days. His average speed was 12 mph (20 kmph), which means that he rode more than 3,200 mi (5,080 km)—about the distance from New York City to San Francisco.

SKI LIFT

Chris Dens of Brainerd, Minnesota, took the sport of waterskiing to new heights by cruising Hartley Lake on 11-ft-tall (3.4-m) stilts! Although he was already an accomplished water-skier—including being a founding member of a local show skiing team—Dens still had to work his way up to the dizzying feat. He started on 3.5-ft (1-m) stilts and then progressed to 6.5-ft-tall (2-m) stilts, before finally—after 20 tries—skiing at a final height of 11 ft (3.4 m).

LONG HAIR

After receiving a bad haircut when she was six years old, Nilanshi Patel, from Gujarat, India, decided not to get it trimmed again—and at age 18 her hair is 6.5 ft (2 m) long.

UNDERWATER WALK

Free-diver Boris Milosic, from Split, Croatia, walked underwater on the floor of a swimming pool for 330 ft (100 m) before needing to surface for air.

COLOSSAL CATCH

On February 14, 2020, Justin Hamlin reeled in a colossal 157-lb (71-kg) paddlefish while fishing on Keystone Lake, Oklahoma. It is believed to be the heaviest paddlefish caught anywhere in the world.

REPLICA SPITFIRE

Bill Pratt, from Hammond, Louisiana, spent nine years building a half-size replica of the famous British World War II fighter plane, the Spitfire, almost entirely from wood in the garage of his home. The wingspan is 23 ft (7 m) across—wider than his garage—so he built it diagonally before taking the various parts of the plane to an airport to be assembled.

BIG BHAJI

Bangladeshi chef Oli Khan made a 386-lb (176-kg) onion bhaji, a type of fritter, in London, England. It took him eight hours to make the big bhaji using 110 gal (500 l) of oil, 11 lb (5 kg) of coriander, and 13.2 lb (6 kg) of garlic and ginger.

FAN FEED

TATER TOT

Nathan Cabrera of Los Angeles, California, shared with us his miniature culinary adventure. After digging up a 0.25-in-long (0.6-cm) potato from his garden, Cabrera wrapped the tiny tuber in foil and baked it. Using an appropriately-sized knife, he then topped the petite potato with a tiny pat of butter, sour cream, and chives. The entire thing fit comfortably on a U.S. quarter and was, according to Cabrera, delicious!

Betsy-Mae says her favorite part of collecting bottles is "digging and getting dirty."

FULL BOTTLE

Betsy-Mae Lloyd, a seven-year-old from Wednesbury, England, has dug up hundreds of antique bottles from historic landfills and sells them in her own shop!

Betsy-Mae's father first took her bottle digging when she was two, and she's been loving it ever since. The pair finds landfill sites by comparing old and new maps, looking for mines that have been filled in. Using this method, they have been able to find bottles dating back as far as the 1870s! They keep their favorites, and Betsy-Mae sells the rest out of her Victorian-style playhouse, which her dad built. She was able to buy herself a new laptop with her earnings!

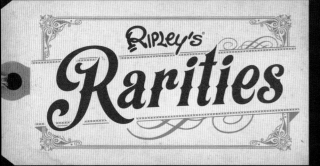

Ripley's Rarities

**Ripley's Exhibit
Cat. No. 168585**

CARD SHARK

Herb Williams of Nashville, Tennessee, created this 9-ft-long (2.7-m) shark out of playing cards. Patterns of royal flushes make up the underside of this poker-faced great white.

**Ripley's Exhibit
Cat. No. 7971**

BEEF BONE DOMINOES

French prisoners of war during the Napoleonic Wars (1803–1815) would hand-carve items out of beef and mutton bones to sell to British military officers as a way to earn money.

ALEX TREBEK CUBE ART

Portrait of late *Jeopardy!* host Alex
Trebek created with 980 mini Rubik's
cubes hand-twisted by New York City
artists Phillip Pollack and Jennifer Loeb.

ALEX TREBEK

From the nightly viewers to the trivia enthusiasts, we've all enjoyed at least one episode of *Jeopardy!* in our lifetime.

Perhaps the most iconic part of the show is not the Daily Double or how contestants must answer in the form of a question, but rather the man who graced the television screen for 36 years, Alex Trebek. The game show legend sadly lost his battle to pancreatic cancer on November 8, 2020, but there is still much to learn about the man who leaves us asking, "Who was Alex Trebek?"

Triple Threat

Alex Trebek was the first game show host to appear on three shows at once. While in his third year as the host of *Jeopardy!*, Trebek also took on NBC's *Classic Concentration* until it ended in September 1991. In February 1991, he took over as the host of NBC's *To Tell the Truth*, making him the host of three simultaneous game shows until that series ended in May.

Trivia Ties

The United States Trivia Association (USTA) was founded in 1979 by future *Jeopardy!* writer Steve Tamerius as a way to bring together the emerging world of trivia. The USTA published a fanzine titled *Trivia Unlimited* until 1983 and also started its own National Trivia Hall of Fame in Lincoln, Nebraska. Robert L. Ripley was the "overwhelming and runaway" choice as its first inductee, according to Tamerius. "Ripley probably contributed more to the widespread interest in trivia, odd and unusual, than any person, past or present."

Record Breaker

Since the first showing of *Jeopardy!* aired on September 10, 1984, Trebek has hosted more than 8,100 episodes! Trebek broke *The Price Is Right* host Bob Barker's Guinness World Record for the "Most Game Show Episodes Hosted by the Same Presenter."

Alex Trebek with Ken Jennings, one of the most successful *Jeopardy!* contestants of all time. Jennings won a record 74 games in a row, winning a total of $3,370,700. He also hosted *Jeopardy!* temporarily, following Trebek's death.

Celebrated Champion

Alex Trebek has won numerous awards in recognition of his talent and demeanor. Trebek was nominated for 34 Daytime Emmy Awards and won seven. He also received a Lifetime Achievement Award from the National Academy of Television Arts and Sciences. As the only post-1960 game show to be awarded, Trebek's work on *Jeopardy!* won him a Peabody Award for "encouraging, celebrating and rewarding knowledge" in 2011.

BIG HAIR, DON'T CARE

Russian artists Asya Kozina and Dmitriy Kozin created a series of wigs made entirely out of paper.

The pieces were inspired by the excessive "art for art's sake aesthetics" of the Baroque and Rococo movements in seventeenth- and eighteenth-century Europe. The duo put a twist on the wigs not only by making them out of paper but by including modern elements like airplanes, Ferris wheels, and skyscrapers. It took about one week to create each headpiece, some of which were featured in a Dolce & Gabbana runway show.

HAIRY POP CULTURE

Long or short, curly or straight, hair has held an honored place in art and media for hundreds of years. Check out some of the strangest hair-related facts from pop culture through the ages!

TALE AS OLD AS TIME
Beauty and the Beast was inspired by the story of Pedro Gonzalez, a sixteenth-century nobleman with hypertrichosis, which results in thick hair growth all over the body.

HAPPY LITTLE HAIRDO
Painter Bob Ross permed his hair to save money on haircuts! He kept the afro after becoming successful because it was so recognizable.

MULTITALENTED
Nearly bald actor Danny DeVito trained as a hairdresser before entering showbusiness.

NO HIPPIES ALLOWED
Men with long hair were not allowed to enter Disneyland until the late 1960s!

NO MORE, NO LESS
Shirley Temple always had exactly 56 curls in her hair!

YOUNG DRUMMER

At age 10, Nandi Bushell, from Ipswich, England, is such a talented drummer that Dave Grohl wrote a song about her, and her drumming videos have racked up nearly 30 million views and won her hundreds of thousands of followers on social media.

GRANITE SCULPTURES

Japanese sculptor Mitsuaki Tanabe spent 10 years traveling back and forth between Japan and Australia, carving images of insects and lizards into large granite boulders. He also carved a 269-ft-long (82-m) wild rice sculpture into rock on a floodplain in Australia's Northern Territory to help promote the grain.

HORROR CARPET

The carpet in bad boy Sid's house in *Toy Story* was deliberately designed with the same hexagonal pattern as the carpet in the 1980 horror movie *The Shining*.

BUDDING ANIMATOR

Jack Nicholson could have ended up drawing Yogi Bear or Scooby-Doo for a living. He was once offered a job as an animator for Hanna-Barbera but turned it down.

When Katy Perry shared a dressing room with Miley Cyrus and Taylor Swift at the Grammys, she asked them both for a lock of their hair, which she carried around in her purse for years after.

1 *Banksia*

Banksia is a genus of around 170 species of shrubs and trees native to Australia. The cones of some species will not open and spread seed unless they have been opened up by the heat of a brush fire!

PYRO PLANTS

Water, sunshine, and soil are the basic needs of any plant, but strangely enough, some plants need fire in order to thrive! Meanwhile, others have adapted to resist fire damage. Here are a few examples of how nature can rise from the ashes.

2 Cogongrass

Cogongrass has an underground system of fire-resistant stems that allows it to bounce back from a wildfire with ease. The aboveground portion of the grass is extremely flammable and burns hotter than most plants, meaning any surrounding flora will also go up in flames, effectively eliminating the grass's competition for resources.

4 Stone Pines

Stone pines and other trees have adapted to fires by "self-pruning" low-growing branches and only growing crowns high above the reach of fire.

3 South African Aloes

Some South African aloes maintain a layer of dead leaves around their stems, which helps insulate the living portion of the plant and protects it from the heat of a fire.

5 Giant Sequoias

Giant sequoias have thick, fire-retardant bark. Massive burn scars on living sequoias are a testament to their resilience. Fire clears the forest floor of dead leaves and allows seeds from sequoia cones to fall onto bare ground, making it possible for them to take root.

FUNKY FLOWER

Hydnora africana is a parasitic plant with a flower that smells like decaying flesh!

Most plants use chlorophyll to absorb nutrients from the sun, and it's this pigment that gives them their green color. But _Hydnora africana_ is not like most plants. The majority of it grows underground and sucks nutrients from the roots of other plants like a vampire! When _Hydnora africana_ is ready to reproduce, it breaks the surface with a strange-looking flower that smells like rotting meat in order to attract flies and beetles, which help spread its pollen.

FLOWER OR ALIEN SPECIES?

GIANT GINKGO

Every autumn, this 1,400-year-old ginkgo tree covers the grounds of Gu Guanyin Temple in China's Shaanxi Province with thousands of yellow leaves. The picturesque transformation attracts tourists and locals alike. Believe it or not, ginkgo trees are considered living fossils, as they have remained unchanged for the last 200 million years!

SPEED ON STILTS

Ben Jacoby of Boulder, Colorado, ran 100 meters in just 13.45 seconds while wearing spring-loaded stilts!

The feat was achieved on October 5, 2018, at the Manhattan Middle School athletics track in Boulder. The footwear makes him more than 12 in (30.5 cm) taller than usual and requires him to be in constant motion; otherwise, he would lose his balance and fall over. Jacoby says he loves being on stilts because it draws people closer to him, even though he is physically further away.

STILETTO SKATER

Wearing a pair of 5-in-high (12.5-cm), stiletto-heeled shoes attached to inline skates, circus performer Bianca Rossini, from Montreal, Canada, skated a distance of 328 ft (100 m) backward in 21.5 seconds.

CARD TOWER

Steady-handed 16-year-old Vishnu Vasu, from Kerala, India, built a 10.6-ft-tall (3.2-m) model of Dubai's Burj Khalifa—the world's tallest building—using 5,450 playing cards. It took him about 5 hours 30 minutes to complete the 33-story structure, which was

BALLOON SCULPTURES

Ryan Tracey, from Omagh, Northern Ireland, can make more than 830 balloon sculptures in an hour, including dogs, swords, and flowers—that's faster than one sculpture every five seconds. He can also make five balloon sculptures in just over 44 seconds while blindfolded.

LONG PUTT

On February 22, 2020, 84-year-old Mary Ann Wakefield sank a 94-ft (29-m) golf putt across the entire length of the court at the University of Mississippi's basketball stadium

TAPE BALL

Students at Eastside Elementary School in Lake City, Florida, created a giant ball of tape measuring 17.9 ft (5.5 m) in circumference. The 2,268-lb (1,030-kg) ball was made from more than 4,000 rolls of tape.

PANCAKE LINE

On Shrove Tuesday 2020, chefs at the Tottenham Hotspur soccer stadium in London, England, cooked up 1,135 pancakes that were arranged into a line that was 429.3 ft (131 m) long. Pancakes are commonly made on Shrove Tuesday as a way

AMBI-ART

Colin Darke of Detroit, Michigan, can draw with both hands at the same time!

The ambidextrous lawyer and artist can illustrate two halves of a portrait or design simultaneously, his right and left hands working independently throughout the remarkable process. Even more impressive is the fact that he is not always mirroring himself, meaning his right and left hands are doing different actions at the same time! To highlight this talent, Darke uses different colored ink or paint for each hand.

IN A NUTSHELL

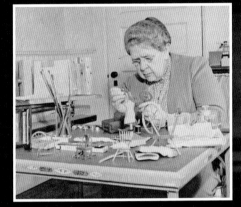

To help train police officers and crime scene investigators, wealthy heiress and forensics pioneer Frances Glessner Lee created the Nutshell Studies of Unexplained Death.

The 1:12 scale replica crime scenes were constructed in the 1940s and 1950s. They depict actual cases down to the smallest detail—functioning lights and locks, as well as perfectly placed cups, bullet holes, food... and corpses. To ensure accuracy, Lee even attended autopsies to properly reproduce the fabrics victims wore. Each diorama cost thousands of dollars and took several months to create. She made 20 of them in all.

Forensics students were given 90 minutes to carefully study the details of the crime scene. The only things they could use were a small flashlight, a magnifying glass, and their own deductive skills to solve the mystery. Lee's dioramas have been so useful in teaching students to pay attention to detail that they are still used today, almost 60 years after her death. For her work, Lee is known as the mother of forensic science.

LIBERTY TORCH

To stop it from breaking in strong gusts, the torch held by the Statue of Liberty was built to sway up to 6 in (15 cm) in winds of 50 mph (80 kmph) or more.

PARKING SPACE

A coveted downtown parking space in Hong Kong sold for $969,000 in 2019—more than three times the cost of the average home in Hong Kong.

DOUBLY LANDLOCKED

The only two double-landlocked countries in the world—nations surrounded completely by other landlocked countries—are Liechtenstein in Central Europe and Uzbekistan in Central Asia.

AFRICAN PLACES

Kanye North and Kanye South (but not Kanye West) are parliamentary constituencies in Botswana, Africa.

FOGGY PLACE

Argentia on the west coast of Newfoundland, Canada, averages 206 days of fog per year.

PERIODIC TABLE

The entire outside wall of a science building at Edith Cowan University in Perth, Western Australia, is decorated with a giant version of the periodic table of the elements. It covers an area of 7,126 sq ft (662 sq m).

BUCHETTA del VINO
WINE WINDOW

WINE WINDOWS

When the city of Florence, Italy, was struck by an outbreak of the bubonic plague in the 1630s, wine sellers kept their distance from customers by installing *buchette del vino*, or wine windows. The holes fell out of use until recently, when precautions against spreading COVID-19 led modern merchants to reopen their wine windows. This time around, cautious customers enjoyed a variety of options other than wine, such as gelato!

BULL CHASE

In the Venezuelan sport of coleo, cowboys on horseback called *llaneros* chase young bulls at high speeds along a narrow pathway and try to drag them to the ground by the tail in the fastest time possible. The sport is more dangerous to humans than the animals because the riders wear very little body protection.

CHEESE CHOICE

At the Pick & Cheese restaurant in London, England, customers choose from 25 varieties of cheese that move past them on a 130-ft-long (40-m) conveyor belt.

UFO WELCOME

The town of St. Paul, Alberta, has its own official UFO landing pad to welcome visitors from other planets. The flat, concrete structure was built in 1967 as part of Canada's centennial celebrations and contains a time capsule to be opened in 2067.

BURGER STACK

The George Pub and Grill in County Durham, England, offers on its menu the Big Ben Number 10—a stack of 10 burgers. The dish contains around 12,000 calories—about five times the recommended daily intake—and owner Craig Harker promises to pay £500 toward the cost of a headstone should anyone die while attempting the challenge.

FISH TANKS

Divers can visit an underwater military museum off the coast of Aqaba, Jordan. Nineteen pieces of decommissioned military machinery—including tanks, a troop carrier, an ambulance, and a helicopter—were sunk up to 92 ft (28 m) down and positioned along coral reefs in battle formation. The equipment also serves as an artificial reef for fish and other sea creatures.

UNDERGROUND OVERNIGHT

China's Intercontinental Shanghai Wonderland puts the luxury in subterranean living, with a 336-room hotel 18 floors beneath the earth's surface.

A low-profile, two-story building with a grass roof greets hotel guests arriving by car. There's not much to see on the surface because 90 percent of the high-end vacation spot sits underground. Constructed in an abandoned quarry, the Wonderland descends 290 ft (88.4 m), culminating in a lake at the bottom. Here, underground suites with a water view pamper the most affluent guests. Taking more than 12 years to complete, the building required 41 new engineering methods during construction.

ODDS AND ENDSTRUMENTS

Artist Ken Butler of Brooklyn, New York, can turn just about anything into a musical instrument.

He has made more than 400 of these hybrid creations, which include objects like chess boards, hockey sticks, coat hangers, instrument cases, shoes, sleds, clocks, tennis rackets, and shovels, among many others. For the most part, Butler's creations are sculptures and aren't intended to be played like actual instruments. However, there are about a dozen or so that he considers "extremely playable," which he uses in live performances, including the very first hybrid he created in 1978—the Axe Violin.

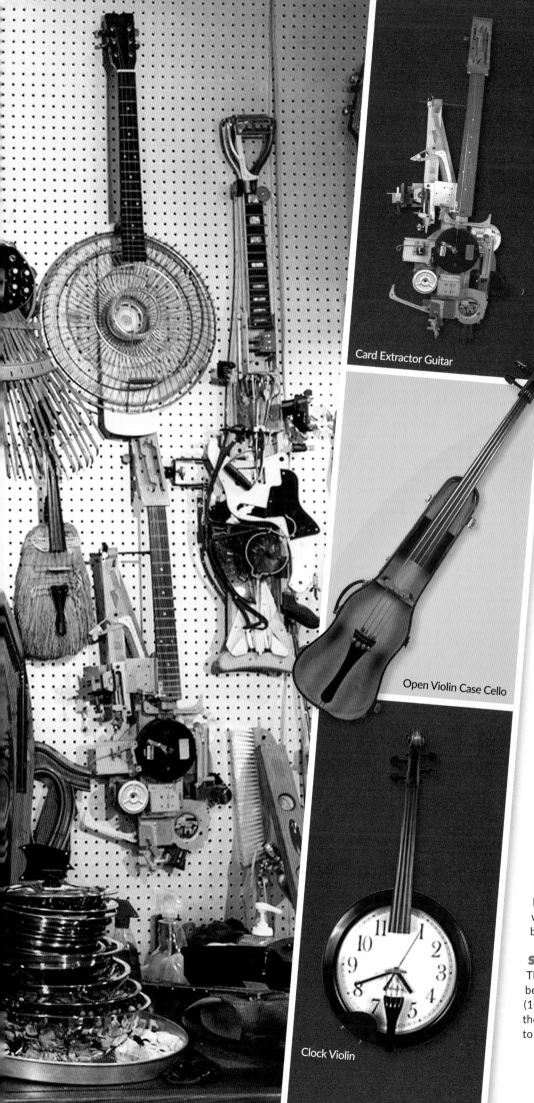

Card Extractor Guitar

Open Violin Case Cello

Clock Violin

ROYAL BOOST
Princess Margaret, sister of Queen Elizabeth II, had the floor of her Rolls-Royce car raised so that she could be seen when she was being chauffeured around the UK.

EXPLOSIVE SECRET
TNT—or trinitrotoluene— was invented in 1863 by German chemist Joseph (Julius) Wilbrand as a yellow dye, and nobody discovered its explosive properties until decades later.

IRONING INJURY
Danish soccer player Michael Stensgaard signed as a goalkeeper for English team Liverpool for £400,000 in 1994, but shortly afterward, he dislocated his shoulder while setting up an ironing board at home and never played a game for the club.

EGG SMASH
On September 24, 2019, more than 136,000 eggs spilled from a tractor-trailer onto Route 125 near Hegins Township, Pennsylvania. The road was closed for several hours while police officers scrambled to clear the mess.

IDENTICAL TWINS
Identical twin babies, Addison and Emma Williams, were delivered by identical twin nurses, Tori Howard and her sister Tara Drinkard, at Piedmont Athens Regional Medical Center in Athens, Georgia, on September 25, 2019.

FLOATING ORANGE
A whole orange will float on water, but a peeled orange will sink. This is because the peel is spongy and contains tiny pockets of air, making the density of the whole orange less than the density of water and therefore allowing it to float.

BLOOD FLOOD
After a drainage mishap with a meat locker next door, the basement of Nick Lestina's house in Bagley, Iowa, flooded with 5 in (12.5 cm) of foul-smelling animal blood and fat.

SMALL STEP
The deepest that anyone has traveled below the surface of the sea is 35,813 ft (10,916 m), which is only 0.0017 percent of the distance needed to complete a journey to the center of the Earth.

CLAWS FULL

A magnificent, multitasking osprey recently stunned Scottish photographers with its simultaneous catch of two fish—one in each set of hooked talons.

Retired air traffic controller Chas Moonie of Ayr, Scotland, captured the extraordinary moment in a handful of photographs. Moonie's shots immortalize the bird of prey pulling two trout from a small fishery's waters near Aviemore in the Scottish Highlands. The photographer has admitted how difficult it is to capture an osprey with one trout, let alone two, attributing it to "being in the right place at the right time."

DOG RESCUE

Sasha Pesic has rescued more than 1,100 abandoned dogs around the city of Nis, Serbia, over the past 10 years and still takes care of 750 of them.

BLOODTHIRSTY

The London Underground system has its own subspecies of mosquito, which has a greater thirst for human blood than its surface-dwelling relatives.

PECKS WOUNDS

In addition to eating flies and ticks off giraffes, hippos, and other African animals, oxpecker birds also eat blood from open wounds. The bird constantly pecks at an animal's wound to keep it open and ensure that more blood flows for the oxpecker to feed on.

BIRD BUDDIES

Like humans, flamingos build friendships that can last for decades. They deliberately stand close to birds they like and avoid those they don't get along with. Flamingo couples that have established such a bond will build nests next to each other and raise their chicks together year after year.

CONSTANT COMPANION

Four-year-old Evelyn "Vadie" Sides survived for two days and nights after becoming lost in the woods in Lee County, Alabama, because her pet dog Lucy stayed by her side throughout the entire ordeal. When a search team finally approached, Lucy barked to alert the rescuers to Evelyn's exact location.

The tongue of the hawk moth can grow up to 14 in (35 cm) long—more than double its body length.

MILLIPEDE MEDICINE

Red-fronted lemurs crush millipedes and then rub the bodily juices over their fur to ward off infection. After using the leggy bugs for medicinal purposes, the lemurs eat them.

TAIL ANCHOR

Unlike most fish that use their tails for swimming, lightweight seahorses wrap their long, prehensile tails around corals, seagrasses, and other objects to keep them from being swept away by strong currents.

KITTEN CARE

In November 2019, a stray dog was discovered by the side of a road in Chatham-Kent, Ontario, Canada, keeping a litter of five abandoned kittens warm.

SEASIDE RIDE

On February 11, 2020, Frank, a four-year-old dachshund, fled while on a country walk with owner Michelle Ballard near Colchester, Essex, England, boarding a route 61 bus and riding 18 mi (29 km) alone to the beach at Clacton-on-Sea.

CAT EPIDEMIC

In 2019, up to 200 feral cats were reported roaming the streets of Garfield, New Jersey.

PLAYTIME

During the UK lockdown in April 2020, a flock of sheep entered the deserted children's play area at Raglan Farm Park in Monmouthshire, Wales, and began riding the merry-go-round.

KELPING OUT

When it comes to spineless beauty, not much compares to the jeweled top snail, a.k.a. the purple-ring snail. This stunner lives mid-level in a high-rise complex of kelp, where every species of snail has its designated space. The jeweled top snails are sandwiched between channeled top snails above and blue top snails below. They never venture far from their "level." If a jeweled top snail gets knocked off or moved? They painstakingly climb back to their attractive kelpmates.

NOTHIN' BUT NET

Amadeus López puts new meaning in the term "slam dunk." The New York City aerialist can usually be seen spinning gracefully on aerial straps—a circus art that requires a large amount of strength, dexterity, and confidence. But it was one of his more unusual tricks that caught our eye. In it, he hangs suspended by his mouth from a basketball hoop and spins two balls, one on the forefinger of each hand. Simultaneously, he shoots a basket with a third ball "thrown" from his foot. Move over, Harlem Globetrotters!

YOUNG ACE

On June 5, 2020, five-year-old William Kelly hit a hole-in-one on the 70-yard 13th hole at The Bridges at Springtree Golf Club in Sunrise, Florida.

MOVIE LOCATIONS

For more than six years, Robin Lachhein and Judith Schneider, from Hofheim, Germany, have been traveling the world recreating more than 70 famous movie scenes in the locations where they were filmed. In similar clothes and poses as the original actors, the couple has honored such classics as *Thelma and Louise* in Utah, *The Devil Wears Prada* in New York, *The Secret Life of Walter Mitty* in Iceland, *Charade* in Paris, and *The Lord of the Rings* in New Zealand.

SAFE CATCH

While magnet fishing on Whitney Lake in South Carolina, six-year-old Knox Brewer reeled in a metal safe that had been stolen from a neighbor's home eight years earlier.

CAP CHAIN

Students at the British International School of Jeddah in Saudi Arabia arranged 323,103 plastic bottle caps into a chain measuring just over 8,984 ft (2,738 m) long.

MEAL DRAWINGS

For more than 30 years, former cook Itsuo Kobayashi, from Saitama, Japan, has drawn a detailed picture of every meal he eats, along with a description of the food, the price, and where it was bought.

BEE MURALS

New York–based muralist Matthew Willey is so fascinated by honeybees that since 2015 he has painted 5,436 bees in 27 separate murals, including on a North Carolina elementary school, the Great Ape House at the Smithsonian's National Zoo in Washington, D.C., and on the roof of an organic farm in Lyons, Nebraska. His eventual aim is to paint 50,000 bees, the number necessary for a healthy hive.

AIRFIELD ODYSSEY

Flying a two-seater Monsun light airplane, Angus and Fiona Macaskill, from Bristol, England, landed at and took off from 71 different UK airfields in 12 hours, covering nearly 690 mi (1,110 km).

HAIR RAISING

A handful of aerialists, including Erin Blaire of New York City, are resurrecting the old circus act known as the hair hang—and, yes, it's as painful as it sounds.

The hair-raising act originated in China, where men and women alike performed it. An early twentieth-century circus poster even depicts a group of Chinese men swinging by their tresses, cross-legged, while drinking tea. Blaire has yet to sip beverages mid-air, but her scalp-tingling performances continue to captivate. The trade secrets necessary to successfully pull off the hair hang remain closely guarded. That said, hairstyle means everything. Each performer braids her tresses differently, never giving away her formula. Rumor has it that some performers spend upward of two hours getting their locks perfectly arrayed before each show.

THE ANCIENT CITY

The world's largest outdoor museum, Muang Boran, covers a whopping 200 acres and showcases 116 examples of architecture, iconic buildings, and monuments.

Also known as Ancient Siam or the Ancient City, Muang Boran sits an hour away from central Bangkok. Featuring recreations of ancient life in Siam, the museum's grounds were designed to reflect modern-day Thailand's shape. From golden stupas to grand pavilions, visitors will find both life-size replicas and scaled-down models of Thai architecture. Scattered among these elaborate temples and structures are ponds, canals, and lakes. Some of the most stunning attractions are Sumeru Temple, situated on an island surrounded by a giant fish, and the green-and-gold roofed Pavilion of the Enlightened, a symbolic representation of the moment 500 monks attained Nirvana.

Guests can buy food and souvenirs at a traditional floating market.

HAIRY PEEPERS

Frankie the dog has veterinarians baffled by the thick tufts of hair growing through both of his eyeballs!

Born on a farm in the United Kingdom, the Jack-Russell-papillon mix was the only puppy in his litter with bushy eyeballs. While making a delivery to the farm, Tracey Smith of Tunbridge Wells, Kent, rescued Frankie from impending euthanasia and took him to the veterinarian for answers. Vets were confounded by his condition, hypothesizing that two cysts behind his eyes cause the fur to grow directly through his eyeballs. Despite the hairy predicament, Frankie has excellent health and retains partial vision. Fortunately, the one-of-a-kind pooch experiences no pain from the condition and doesn't even need to have his ocular tresses trimmed.

LITTLE BULL

Humphrey, a five-year-old bull owned by the Gardner family of Kalona, Iowa, stands just 26.6 in (66.5 cm) tall. When the Gardner family bought the miniature Zebu bull in 2017, he was so small they assumed he was a calf, only to discover Humphry was two years old and therefore fully grown.

HUMAN FLESH

Two feral cats broke into a research facility in Whitewater, Colorado, and ate the flesh from the shoulders and arms of human corpses. The Colorado Mesa University's Forensic Investigation Research Station had left more than 40 human bodies outside to document what happens to decaying human flesh, but the cats penetrated the 10-ft-high (3-m) wire-topped fence, which also extends 2 ft (0.6 m) below ground, and feasted on two of the corpses, chewing right to the bone. One cat returned to eat the same corpse for 35 nights straight.

CLUMSY TORTOISE

A tortoise started a house fire in Essex, England, after knocking over a heat lamp, which then ignited its bedding.

BLACK MEAT

The Ayam Cemani chicken not only has black feathers and a black beak, it also has black bones, black organs, and even black meat. Its meat is said to possess mystical powers by locals in the chicken's native Indonesia.

CRICKET PLAGUE

To try and fight off twice-yearly plagues of Mormon crickets, residents of Tuscarora, Nevada, played loud rock music by Led Zeppelin and the Rolling Stones. The 3-in-long (7.5-cm) bugs march in columns up to 2 mi (3.2 km) long and 1 mi (1.6 km) wide, destroying crops and invading homes.

MAMMOTH TOOTH

Twelve-year-old Jackson Hepner found a fossilized tooth of a woolly mammoth while playing in a Millersburg, Ohio, creek in 2019. The tooth is around 7 in (17.5 cm) long, weighs 6 lb (2.7 kg), and dates back 10,000 years!

THREE ANTLERS

On November 10, 2019, in Michigan's Upper Peninsula, photographer Steve Lindberg took a one-in-a-million picture of a three-antlered deer. In addition to an impressive five-point antler, the large buck had two smaller antlers growing out of its skull, side by side.

HURRICANE SURVIVOR

A dog was given the name Miracle when it was rescued alive after spending almost a month trapped in the rubble of a collapsed building in Marsh Harbor in the Bahamas following Hurricane Dorian. He had survived by drinking rainwater.

HONEY ROASTED

Bee-lieve it or not, to protect their hive from being attacked by Asian giant hornets (a.k.a. "murder hornets"), Japanese honeybees will smother and cook the invaders alive! Although out-sized by the hornet, the bees have numbers on their side. Hundreds of workers will gather around the intruder and vibrate their wings to raise the temperature inside the "bee ball" to up to 115°F (46°C) for as long as an hour! This heated act of defense shortens the lifespan of the workers, but it also protects the rest of the hive from being decapitated and eaten!

BIG BIRD

Sculptor Farvardin Daliri, from Townsville, Australia, built a 28-ft-long (8.5-m), 15-ft-tall (4.6-m), electrified laughing kookaburra. The oversized bird has a steel frame covered in painted bamboo straws (to replicate feathers) and a fiberglass beak. Daliri installed an old car battery and motor to operate the bird's beak, and inside its body, he placed an amplified recording of the sounds of a real kookaburra. The sculpture is welded to a trailer and travels around Queensland, where it attracts the attention of children and adults alike, plus real kookaburras, even though it is nearly 20 times their size.

Ripley's Rarities

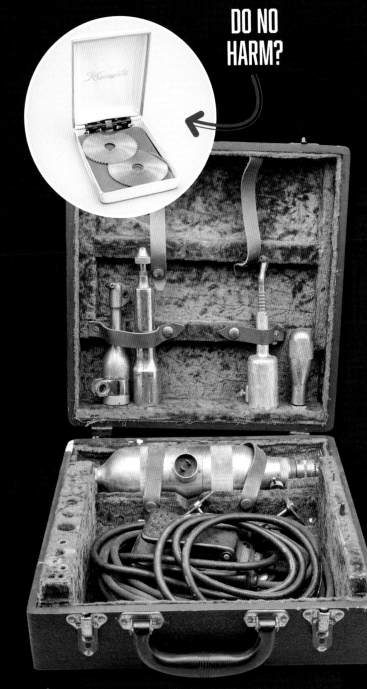

DO NO HARM?

Ripley's Exhibit
Cat. No. 174246

MEDICAL SAW KIT

Oscillating saw from the early 1900s that could have been used for a variety of medical purposes, including sawing through bone or plaster casts.

Ripley's Exhibit
Cat. No. 10039, 10040

PESTLE DOLLS

A thrifty pioneer woman of the mid-nineteenth century originally used these pestles to grind medicine and later painted them as dolls for her children to play with.

Ripley's Exhibit
Cat. No. 174066

HUMAN HEART

An actual human heart preserved through the process of plastination, during which water and fats are replaced with plastics and the tissue remains untouched.

REAL HUMAN HEART!

NAIL SANDWICH

In Surat, India, nine men lay down stacked atop one another in a human tower with a bed of long, sharp metal nails between each person. The bottom man in the bed-of-nails sandwich, who had to bear the weight of the other eight, was martial artist Vispy Kharadi.

196 MARATHONS

British endurance athlete Nick Butter ran 196 marathons, one in every country of the world, in 22 months. He covered more than 5,130 mi (8,208 km) and took a total of 5.1 million steps. He started in Toronto, Canada, in January 2018 and went on to compete in races in such diverse locations as the Sahara and Antarctica. In the course of his adventures, he broke his elbow and was shot at, hit by a car, and bitten by a dog.

REPLICA BATMOBILE

Brian Hendler, of Chicago, Illinois, spent four years building a life-sized replica of the Batmobile. The 22-ft-long (6.7-m) vehicle has a Boeing jet engine in the back and can pick itself up and spin 360 degrees.

EXOSKELETON SUIT

Walking with the aid of a robotic exoskeleton suit, Adam Gorlitsky, who has been paralyzed from the waist down since a car crash in 2005, completed his hometown Charleston Marathon in South Carolina in 33 hours 50 minutes 24 seconds. He started on the night of Thursday, January 9, 2020, and crossed the finish line on the morning of Saturday, January 11, without taking any breaks for sleep.

DELAYED GOLD

Thirty-eight years after winning a silver medal in swimming as a 12-year-old at the Southeast Asian Games, Singapore's Christina Tham went one better by winning gold at the 2019 games in underwater hockey.

HUGE HAIR

Joe Grisamore, of Park Rapids, Minnesota, has been growing his hair in a mohawk style since 2013, and six years later it stood an incredible 42 in (1.05 m) tall.

SUPER SCHNITZEL

At the 2019 Schnitzel Fest in Mengkofen, Germany, cooks made a 2,663-lb (1,209-kg) schnitzel that covered an area of 753.5 sq ft (70 sq m)—almost half the size of a volleyball court. Containing the meat from 400 chops, 4,000 eggs, and 551 lb (250 kg) of bread crumbs and fried in 3,700 gal (14,000 l) of oil, the monster schnitzel served nearly 5,000 people.

FAVORITE RESTAURANT

Mark Mendenhall, of San Diego, California, ate at the Carmel Mountain branch of Chick-fil-A for 114 days straight (except Sundays, when the chain is closed).

TIRING TIME

Roy West, from Hampshire, England, has a collection of 5,000 clocks. Twice a year—at the beginning and end of British Summer Time (Daylight Savings Time)—it takes him more than five hours to reset each one by hand.

British siblings Jackson and Freya Houlding climbed a nearly 11,000-ft-tall (3,350-m) mountain, despite being only three and seven years old, respectively.

The pair were led and, in Jackson's case, carried up the Swedish mountain Piz Badile by their parents Leo and Jessica Houlding. The ascent made Freya the youngest person to climb the mountain unaided and Jackson the youngest person to make it to the top. It took the family several days to complete, and they spent the fourth night in a cliffside hut, with a massive drop about 3 ft (1 m) away from the door!

NEW HEIGHTS

JACKSON IS ONLY 3 YEARS OLD!

FIRE FESTIVAL

One night a year, people in the small town of Nejapa, El Salvador, gather in the streets to throw flaming, fuel-drenched balls at each other!

The reason for the commotion is the Bolas de Fuego, or "balls of fire," festival, which commemorates the 1922 volcanic eruption that nearly wiped out the entire town. Local legend attributes the explosion to a fight between their patron saint San Jeronimo and the Devil. Participants dressed in masks and face paint split into two groups and spend the night reenacting the duel. Medical professionals are on standby, but surprisingly there haven't been any major injuries reported in all the years of celebrations.

TRAPPED TONGUE

While trying to lick out the last few drops, a seven-year-old boy from Hanover, Germany, got his tongue stuck in a glass juice bottle. After his parents unsuccessfully tried to twist it off and his tongue started to swell and turn blue, they took him to a hospital, where doctors eventually removed the bottle by pumping air into the bottleneck.

ROYAL HELP

After five-year-old Savannah Hart, from Adelaide Hills, South Australia, accidentally left Harriet, her toy monkey, behind on a visit to Buckingham Palace, London, she wrote to Queen Elizabeth II and Harriet was put on the next flight home.

> A wheel that fell from a helicopter in mid-air crashed through the roof of Linda Taylor-Whitt's home in Lynwood, Illinois, and lodged in the bathroom ceiling.

HEAD BITE

Twelve days after colliding with another player during a school soccer game in Setubal, Portugal, a 14-year-old boy had one of the player's teeth removed from his skull. The tooth was embedded in a 2-in (5-cm) cut on the side of his head.

VOMIT EXPERIMENTS

In an attempt to prove that yellow fever was not a contagious disease, Stubbins Ffirth, an early-nineteenth-century trainee doctor in Philadelphia, drank glasses full of black vomit obtained from a yellow fever patient. He also poured fresh black vomit into self-made cuts on his arms, dribbled it into his eyeballs, and fried vomit before inhaling the fumes, all without ever getting sick. (This is because yellow fever is transmitted by mosquitos.)

PLANE LOVE

Michele Köbke, from Berlin, Germany, has been in love with a 40-ton Boeing 737-800 passenger airplane for more than six years. She calls it "Schatz," the German word for "darling," and keeps a large model of the plane

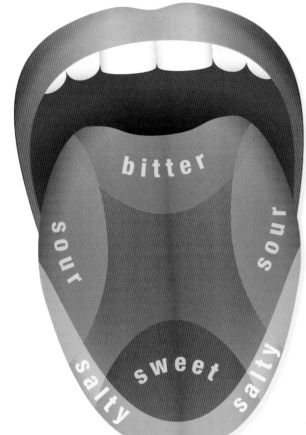

 **FOOD EDITION**

Sometimes a misconception gets repeated so often that many end up believing it's a fact.

Here at Ripley's, we like to call that an "Or Not!" because you can't always "Believe It!" Grab a snack and chew on these food-related Or Not! facts.

1 Flavor Town

Do tongues contain different regions for sampling flavors like sweet, bitter, and salty? Nope—so-called "tongue mapping" remains a pseudo-science, debunked by chemosensory scientists many decades ago.

2 An Apple a Day

Sorry, folks, but an apple a day doesn't keep the doctor away! Sure, consuming any fruit comes with nutritional benefits, but researchers note no appreciable drop in physician visits among daily apple nibblers.

3 Wet Your Whistle

Some researchers now believe drinking eight glasses of eight ounces of water each day is overkill. Instead of following the 8 × 8 rule, they suggest paying attention to your body's natural thirst.

4 See You Later

If you've ever swallowed a piece of gum, we've got good news for you. Contrary to urban legend, gum moves through your digestive tract and gets eliminated like food and does not stay in your stomach for seven years.

5 The Five-Second Rule Breaker

We've all taken a nosedive to save food from the floor, but does the "five-second rule" hold up? A two-year study in 2016 concluded that no matter how fast you rescue food from the floor, it can still be laced with bacteria.

6 Fortunate Beginnings

Far from being Chinese or American in origin, fortune cookies were actually introduced by Japanese immigrants at their San Francisco bakeries as *senbei*, or "crackers."

7 Everlasting Food

If you're wagering on a meal from McDonald's to last long enough for you to survive a zombie apocalypse, think again. Mickey D's food is no less prone to rotting than a home-cooked meal.

8 Nap Time

"Turkey Day" comes once a year, delivering doses of drowsiness thanks to the tryptophan in turkey, right? Wrong! Carb-loading and over-eating are the culprits behind Thanksgiving's famous post-meal snoozes.

Gingerbread Venom

SWEET SCULPTURES

Move over, gingerbread house builders! You'll never view Yuletide cookies the same way after seeing the pop culture sculptures of artist Caroline Eriksson.

Based in Oslo, Norway, Eriksson crafts everything from aliens and Darth Vader to human skulls from the pepperkaker sweet treat. Her artwork is so realistic, few would willingly sink their teeth into her movie-inspired masterpieces like Groot from *Guardians of the Galaxy* or antihero Venom, dripping with sugary saliva.

I AM GROOT!

Gingerbread Xenomorph

FAKE OUT

Arachnophobes can relax—this hairy spider is actually a caterpillar! Throughout the Americas, you can find the oddly named and strangely shaped monkey slug caterpillar. The larvae of the hag moth, its underside consists of slimy suction cup–like legs while the top half of its body is decorated with long, hairy arms that curl out, imitating the look of a tarantula.

APPROPRIATE NAME

In December 2019, firefighters in Graham, Washington, rescued a horse that had become tangled in an active, fallen power line. Appropriately, the horse's name was Touch of Generator.

DOG MAYOR

Murfee the therapy dog was elected mayor of Fair Haven, Vermont, in 2020, beating the incumbent goat, Mayor Mara Lincoln, and K-9 Sammy, a police dog.

POLAR GREETING

Polar bears greet each other by touching noses. They will also approach another polar bear that is eating and touch its nose to ask permission to share the meal.

JUMBO HANGOVER

A herd of 14 elephants raided a village in Yunnan Province, China, in search of food and got drunk on corn wine instead. Two male elephants passed out in a nearby tea garden.

ALARM SILENCER

A woman in São Paulo, Brazil, was repeatedly late for work because her cat Joaquim secretly turned her phone alarm off each morning by hitting the screen with its paw when the device began vibrating on the bedside table.

BLUE BLOOD

A rare tree native to New Caledonia's rainforests, *pycnandra acuminata* boasts a rare blue-green, sap-like fluid containing up to 25 percent nickel. In other words, the tree literally bleeds metal! How does it work? These plants have the unique ability to collect large quantities of nickel from the soil, which gives these organisms their turquoise-colored sap.

BOOTYFUL BUGS

The nymph stage of planthopper insects is a sight to behold!

There are thousands of species of planthoppers, and many go through a fabulous phase during their lifespan in which they sprout curious growths from their rear ends. These extravagant tails are made of water-repellent wax and protect the itty-bitty nymphs from predators through the art of distraction. Among some species, the stunning, multicolored fan-like tails also help the insect slow down when falling through the air, like a makeshift parachute!

Using a Dremel drill tool and a pure white car as a "canvas," London artist Claudia De Sabe has created the world's first tattooed car.

Lexus developed the tattooed car concept to pay homage to the traditional artistry and fine craftsmanship of Japanese tattooing. De Sabe decorated the vehicle with sweeping images, including a koi carp design spanning its length. She used the Dremel to expose the metal beneath the white, followed by 1.3 gal (5 l) of high-quality paint to bring out the details. Finishing gold-leaf touches created highlights, rendering the vehicular artwork three-dimensional.

ROLL OUT

Aladdin would go gaga over the Azerbaijan Carpet Museum in Baku. Housed in a long, narrow building shaped like a rolled-up carpet, the museum appears genuinely enchanted. Designed by Austrian architect Franz Janz, the museum took six years to build, with workers completing it in 2014. The impressive exterior shell contains elaborate decorative patterns evocative of the significant woven pieces displayed on the curved walls inside.

HIDDEN CORPSE

After English literary critic William Hazlitt died in 1830, his landlady, eager to rent out his room again as soon as possible, hid his body under a bed and showed prospective tenants around the London apartment while his corpse was still there.

MODEL TRAINS

Musician Rod Stewart spent 26 years creating a 1,500-sq-ft (140-sq-m) model train layout in his Los Angeles home based on an American industrial city of the 1940s. He started work on it in 1993 and used to take tools, paints, and kits with him on tour so that he could pursue his hobby between concerts. Sometimes he would even book an extra hotel room to serve as a modeling workshop.

DOUBLE TAKE

Actresses Keira Knightley and Natalie Portman looked so alike in full makeup while filming *Star Wars: The Phantom Menace* that even their own mothers had difficulty telling them apart on set.

Finnish musician Tuomas Holopainen topped the charts in his home country with a concept album based entirely on a Scrooge McDuck graphic novel.

MOVIE BAN

Monty Python's Life of Brian was banned in the Welsh town of Aberystwyth for 30 years. The ban was only lifted in 2009 when Sue Jones-Davies, who played Judith Iscariot in the film, was elected mayor of Aberystwyth.

HELICOPTER FEAR

Filming *The Lord of the Rings: The Fellowship of the Ring* required cast and crew to fly to remote mountain locations in New Zealand by helicopter. But British actor Sean Bean, who played Boromir, was scared of flying and often chose to make a two-hour hike on foot and in full costume to the set.

EARLY ROLES

Future Cuban leader Fidel Castro appeared in two 1946 Hollywood movies as a background extra. He played a poolside spectator in the romantic comedy *Easy to Wed* and sang and danced in *Holiday in Mexico*.

COBAIN CHECK

An uncashed royalty check for $26.57 issued to Kurt Cobain and dated March 6, 1991—six months before Nirvana released their worldwide best-selling album *Nevermind*—was discovered in 2019 folded inside a used record collection at the Easy Street Records store in Seattle, Washington.

Like many people, Matthew Van Vorst of Astoria, New York, took up a new hobby while in lockdown due to COVID-19. However, he's probably the only person who started sculpting cheese—at least to the degree and detail that he is able to achieve!

While Van Vorst has dabbled in art in the past, he tells us his "Cuttin' the Cheese" project is his first venture into sculpting. It started with a vaguely couch-shaped block of cheese that made his co-quarantiners laugh and evolved into an ongoing series of sculptures depicting a variety of subjects, from sandwiches to suitcases. The Ripley's team had a lot of questions, and who cheddar to ask than the artist himself?

Q: Other than cheese and the tools used for carving, do you use any other materials to make your pieces?
A: Nope! Only cheese!

Q: How do you choose what kind of cheese to carve?
A: Some cheeses are better than others, depending on the subject. Cheddar is great for gouging and carving designs into. It has some give and is somewhat forgiving if you slip up. Swiss and Jarlsberg hold together well and are wonderful for sculpts with big holes in them, as they won't fall apart as easily. But Parmigiano-Reggiano has to be my favorite to work with. You can scrape it, cut it, slice it, and make really fine details. It holds together well, and, let's be honest, it's the most delicious.

Q: What has been your favorite or most difficult piece to date?

A: So far, my most difficult is also my favorite: "Feet Slippers in Sharp Cheddar." The idea came from an art piece by Emily Blythe Jones, which was a pair of realistic feet slippers made of latex. I thought it was so much fun that I wanted to do a response in cheese. The difficulty came from it being such an organic piece. It's not like a building or some angular shape that is easily measurable. Working from a human form means that there's movement, life, variation. It's difficult to capture that effectively, but it came out perfectly. It's deliciously weird.

Q: What do you do with the sculptures after you've completed them?

A: They definitely get eaten! Of course, I have to photograph them. But, then, they're eaten. I'm sure it's not healthy of a habit... but there's just always so much cheese in my fridge! Who could say no?

"It's deliciously weird."

Q: What tips would you give to an aspiring cheese artist?

A: Refrigeration! And air conditioning. The biggest difficulty with working in cheese is that it warms up so quickly. And once cheese is warm, it becomes awful to work with. It sweats, gets soft, and falls apart. So, where a clay sculpture might take a few hours, a cheese sculpture can take days because you have to keep wrapping the cheese and putting it back in the fridge.

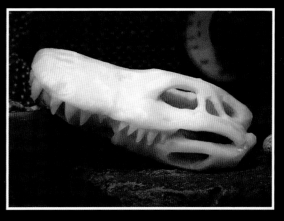

Most of Van Vorst's sculptures are made from a single, solid block of cheese, ranging from 2 to 6 in (5 to 15 cm) in length.

THE PROCESS

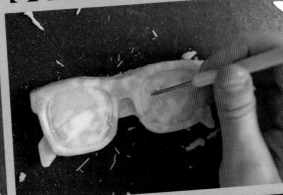

SCRATCH-OFF ART

James Owen Thomas of Pateley Bridge, England, creates works of art out of scratch-off lottery tickets.

The project was born out of Thomas's passion for recycling and disdain for litter. Many of the tickets used in his pieces are found on the streets or in parks, discarded by lotto losers. The multitude of bright colors meant to lure in players give Thomas a large and vibrant palette to work with.

LOTTO LUCK

It's said that you are more likely to be struck by lightning than win the lottery, but don't tell that to the folks on this list, who have won big in lucky ways!

GAS LUCK

In July 2020, a gas station clerk in Eastpointe, Michigan, accidentally gave a man a $20 scratch-off card instead of the $10 card and change he requested. Luckily, the man decided to keep the $20 card because he ended up winning $2 million!

BIRTHDAY JACKPOT

Dennis Ressler of Boiling Springs, South Carolina, won a $1 million lottery jackpot on his birthday!

LUCKY COOKIE

In 2005, a fortune cookie company printed winning lottery numbers, leading to 110 wins!

REPEATED LUCK

On the same night that Anthony McIntyre Sr. of Georgetown, Kentucky, had told his neighbors about winning $100,000 off a scratch-off lottery ticket three years earlier, he bought another ticket and won $100,000 again!

A PIECE OF PRIDE AND PREJUDICE

In celebration of the 25th anniversary of the BBC's *Pride and Prejudice* series, UKTV Play's Drama Channel commissioned food artist Michelle Wibowo to craft a life-sized cake of Colin Firth's Mr. Darcy.

Long considered a treat by Austen fanatics, Colin Firth looks downright tasty as the ultimate romantic hero—sponge cake, frosting, and all. How did Wibowo achieve this confectionary marvel? The architect-turned-baker spent three weeks and 200 hours crafting her 6-ft (1.8-m) Darcy dessert. She started with a metal skeleton to which she applied Victoria sponge cake and chocolate ganache. Topped with vanilla buttercream and fondant icing, the dessert appears disarmingly dashing.

BLUE LOOK

Lhouraii Li, a makeup artist from Bradford, England, has been painting her face and hands blue almost every day for more than two years. Inspired by aliens, she thinks a blue complexion suits her personality and makes her feel more confident. She wants to become permanently blue but because she fears she may be allergic to tattoos, she relies on face paint instead.

CHILD SURGEON

India's Akrit Pran Jaswal performed his first surgery when he was only seven years old. Known in his village as a medical genius, he agreed to separate the fingers of an eight-year-old girl who had been badly burned as a toddler. Her fingers had melted together, but the one-hour surgery he performed for free greatly improved her quality of life. He was later accepted into medical school at Punjab University at age 11.

PRISON CONVERT

Graham Skidmore, from Worcestershire, England, converted an old police van that had been used to transport prisoners to court into a summer house for his wife. He paid £250 for the van, and it cost him another £750 to remove the five cells and toilet, but he kept the heavy doors and the hatch through which the driver talked to the prisoners. All in all, the project was a bargain when compared to the £42,000 he had been quoted for a new sunroom.

DIRT COLLECTION

The shelves of Bruce Jackson's home in Wilson, North Carolina, are lined with more than 360 baby food jars containing dirt from interesting or historic places around the world. They include dirt from John F. Kennedy's grave, the Alamo, the Leaning Tower of Pisa, Buckingham Palace, the Berlin Wall, Graceland, and Gettysburg.

EGG STACK

Using no adhesives, Mohammed Muqbel, a 20-year-old Yemeni man living in Kuala Lumpur, Malaysia, balanced three chicken eggs on top of each other in a vertical stack. He has been balancing eggs since he was six and says the secret is to identify each egg's center of mass, making sure these are precisely aligned when stacked.

FISHING FAMILY

While fishing in Old Hickory Lake, Tennessee, nine-year-old Coye Price, who weighs just 55 lb (25 kg), caught a giant sturgeon that weighed 80 lb (36 kg). It took him 15 minutes to get the fish on the boat before it was released back into the water. He is the third child in his family to reel in a giant fish, following his 11-year-old sister Caitlin, who caught a 40-lb (18-kg) striper, and his eight-year-old sister Farrah, who landed a 58-lb (26-kg) blue catfish.

ON A ROLL

Vasilisa Maslova is on a roll with her gravity-defying skating tricks. The Belarussian freestyle slalom rollerblader won the world title in the Netherlands in 2018, and she has the moves to prove it. Not only can she effortlessly complete a slalom course while freestyle dancing, but she can also do it on one leg while skating backward in a single-wheel squat. Talk about fitness goals!

WORK-LIFE BALANCE

Dan Wasdahl of Massillon, Ohio, is able to juggle, hula-hoop, and balance a spinning plate on a stick in his mouth, all while standing on a moving platform. Oh, and it is all on fire!

The 65-year-old specializes in "combination tricks" and is able to perform a variety of different stunts at the same time. But Wasdahl isn't a full-time circus performer. Rather, he is a medical doctor working at Northeast Ohio Medical University as an associate professor of pathology. Where others scrapbook or make model airplanes, Wasdahl keeps a sometimes literal work-life balance by participating in the Wizbang Circus Theatre and managing the 9th Avenue Street Circus in his free time.

Ripley's Exhibit
Cat. No. 168548

CD ART

Sean Avery of Australia gives new life to trashed compact discs by turning them into art, such as this peregrine falcon. He cuts the CDs into shape with scissors before gluing them together onto a wire frame.

California artist Russell Powell developed a style of painting he calls "handstamping," in which he paints his palm before stamping it onto a paper canvas. This guitar collage is made up of 16 famous guitarists, including Jimi Hendrix, Eric Clapton, Eddie Van Halen, Slash, Chuck Berry, Kurt Cobain, and others.

Ripley's Exhibit
Cat. No. 172698

BROKEN RECORD

A split portrait by artist Ed Chapman of Manchester, England, of rap legends Tupac Shakur and The Notorious B.I.G. created with shattered record pieces. The artwork is 4 ft (1.2 m) tall.

RECEIPT REBELLION

Bavarian pastry shop Bäckerei Ways decorates doughnuts with edible receipts! The fondant topping is a cheeky means of protest to a new law in Germany that requires shops to provide receipts for every exchange. Critics claim the law produces an unnecessary amount of waste, since most receipts are printed on thermal paper that cannot be recycled. A hit, the bakery went from producing 300 doughnuts one week to 900 the next, according to the shop's lead baker, Ludovic Gerboin.

BUGGY BREAKFAST

The Vietnamese dish *chả rươi* looks like a mix between a pancake and an omelet, but it contains a special ingredient that defies the imagination for most Western palates: sandworms. A popular street food in north Vietnam, this delicacy is a staple of cities like Hanoi. Served with a fish sauce, it has a meaty texture and savory fragrance. Sandworms live in the northern wetlands and are harvested during the fall. They can be used frozen or fresh, although locals swear by fresh sandworms for the best *chả rươi*.

BRICK OVEN

Iouri Petoukhov of Canada has combined his passion for pizza and love of LEGO into the ultimate plastic-brick, pie-making machine!

Using only LEGO, he and his son, Michael, have crafted a gourmet gadget that can generate a full pizza, from sauce to cheese, peppers, and sausage. It even slices the pizza once it's finished baking! Petoukhov's cooking contraption is just one of several jaw-dropping creations he and Michael have crafted under the name "The Brick Wall."

1 Snakes

Snakes don't dislocate their jaws to eat their food! Unlike mammals, a snake's lower jawbone is not fused to the upper jawbone, allowing them to swallow prey much larger than themselves.

...OR NOT! ANIMAL EDITION

Sometimes a misconception gets repeated so often that many end up believing it's a fact.

At Ripley's, we like to call that an "Or Not!" because you can't always "Believe It!" Here are some of our favorite animal-related Or Not! facts.

2 Toads

Touching a toad will not give you warts! While the amphibians may look warty, the bumps on their bodies are just that—bumps! There are five types of warts, but none of them are caused by toads or frogs.

3 Birds

Touching a baby bird will not make its mother abandon it. The smell of a human is not enough to override a mother bird's instinct to care for her offspring. That said, if you see a baby bird hopping around, it's probably learning to fly, and you should leave it alone.

4 Black Panthers

Black panthers are not an actual species! The term "black panther" doesn't refer to a separate species. It describes coat color! There are black-coated jaguars, leopards, and other big cats, many of which are referred to as "black panthers."

5 Opossums

Opossums don't actually play dead when they're threatened. Instead, they involuntarily enter a catatonic state where their bodies go completely limp and their breathing appears to stop.

WHAT'S THE MATA MATA?

South America's mata mata turtle remains the king of camouflage, blending effortlessly with the environment and even hiding an unknown species!

The mata mata turtle *(Chelus fimbriata)* is an expert at disguising itself among the rocks, algae, and plant debris of the Amazon basin. From its wedge-shaped head and wide mouth to its tiny eyes, the reptile looks positively alien. Skin flaps, wart-like tubercles, and a knobby, algae-covered shell make it the equivalent of a walking plant. Upon noticing slight differences among mata mata populations in the Amazon, scientists conducted genetic testing, revealing *Chelus orinocensis*, a previously undocumented species!

THE MATA MATA USES ITS NOSE LIKE A SNORKEL!

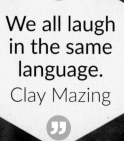

> "We all laugh in the same language.
> Clay Mazing

Clay Mazing entertains an orphan near the U.S.–Mexico border.

EMERGENCY CIRCUS

It's said that laughter is the best medicine, so for Clay Mazing of New Orleans, Louisiana, it made perfect sense to create the Emergency Circus—a group of performers who use their talents to bring joy and laughter to people all around the world!

The group has performed at refugee camps and hospitals, as well as for people affected by natural disasters and homeless communities. In 2020, they comforted their hometown of New Orleans as it suffered an outbreak of COVID-19. In keeping with the theme, they used their "Sh'zambulance" to bring Circ-A-Grams to citizens in need of a distraction and a laugh—all at a safe distance and no cost. They even offered virtual performances for people who weren't local! Emergency Circus shows exclude knife juggling, bullwhip stunts, clown acts, and more! Ripley's spoke with Clay Mazing to find out more about the Emergency Circus.

Catalina Paz, Severin Steensen, Clay Mazing, Maya Pen, Julia Cev, Lucy Ray, and María Daniela Ochoa from their "Bridge the Border" tour in 2019.

Q: What inspired you to create Circ-A-Grams during the COVID-19 pandemic?
A: One night during quarantine, I ordered pizza delivery, and it dawned on me that if pizza can be delivered safely, then I could deliver a circus act door-to-door safely, too. So I created a hotline (1-NOW-CIRCUS-1) and made a cheesy commercial offering my services by donation. It worked well; I've been able to perform countless shows to quarantined people all over New Orleans and around the country.

The Sh'zambulance

Q: What can someone attending an Emergency Circus performance expect?
A: Every Emergency Circus show is catered to the area and crisis the people are faced with. In Puerto Rico, for instance, we developed an act where two clowns performed a luchador wrestling act between Hurricane Maria and El Yunque, a rainforest on the island that the indigenous people believed protected them from hurricanes. Of course, El Yunque won the battle and the children could celebrate the defeat of the traumatizing event they recently went through.

> **"There's no telling how the love and joy we share expands to ripple effect the world."**

Q: Where has the Emergency Circus performed? Does the Sh'zambulance always go with you?
A: We have performed in more than 30 countries around the world. We don't bring the Sh'zambulance across the sea, but we have done a number of tours along the U.S.–Mexico border. Nothing beats the joyful yet confused look on the face of an orphan in rural Mexico when a brightly colored ambulance shows up and a bunch of clown superheroes pop out of it!

Justin Therrien clowning around with orphaned children on the U.S.–Mexico border.

Moniek de Leeuw plays violin as Clay Mazing lassos for Syrian refugees in Greece.

Q: What are some experiences that stick out to you?

A: Some of my favorite moments are the parades. Often, we gather folks for a performance by parading through the area. We let the children lead the parade, and we teach them all a sing-along song, play instruments, and pass out shakers and noisemakers. It's so heartwarming to see faces pop out of cardboard shacks or UNICEF tents and transform from confusion to laughter. People grab their shoes and join the parade. The whole energy of the camp changes into a celebration. People from different countries, ethnicities, and religions all clap along and watch the circus. It proves that we all laugh in the same language.

Q: What is the most surprising reaction that you've gotten from your performances?

A: That's a hard question, but there is a story that comes to mind. When I was in Tijuana last year, I performed at a center that housed only adult men. I was nervous that my antics might not be appreciated without children present, but I was shocked at how involved and grateful the audience was. They really did become like children, and they thanked me profusely after the show, saying they really needed to laugh like that. It reaffirmed my belief in the importance of this work.

Emergency Circus clowns bringing laughter to an orphanage in Mexico.

NATURE'S DESSERT

This fruit isn't rotten—it's a black sapote, a.k.a. chocolate pudding fruit! It is native to Mexico and Central America, but can be grown in other places around the world. Unlike most fruits, this one isn't ripe until it is soft, squishy, and oozing juices! The color and texture is just like that of a thick chocolate custard. Some people eat it right out of the peel with a spoon, while others get creative and mix it with spices, use it in baking, or turn it into ice cream!

Among more than 100 different flavors created by Japanese soft drinks manufacturer Kimura are fish egg, pickled plum, curry, potato chip, and eel cola.

POPULAR NAMES

About 45 percent of South Koreans have one of three surnames—Kim, Lee, or Park (Pak). For many years, it was illegal in South Korea to marry someone with the same surname.

WEIRD FLAVORS

Maria del Carmen Pilapaña owns a stall in Quito, Ecuador, that sells guinea pig–flavored ice cream. Guinea pig is a traditional dish in several Latin American countries. She also serves ice cream in mushroom and beetle flavors.

LONELY TREE

The Tree of Ténéré, a solitary acacia located in the Sahara, was once the only tree for 250 mi (400 km). It stood in total isolation for decades until an allegedly drunk driver knocked it down in 1973.

PRISON KNITTERS

Inmates in Brazil's high-security Arisvaldo de Campos Pires prison can earn reduced sentences by taking up knitting for fashion designer Raquel Guimaraes. They get one day off their sentence for every three days that they knit.

FREE FLIGHTS

To promote its Green Week in August 2019, U.S.-based Frontier Airlines offered free flights to people with the last name Green or Greene.

CRIMINAL TOMB

The extravagant tomb of convicted criminal Antonio "El Tonto" in Pinos Puente, Spain, features a life-size bronze statue of him and a full-size replica of an Audi Q5, the car he used to carry out a series of daring truck hijackings.

SWISS TEST

Anyone in Switzerland who fails their driver's test more than three times has to undergo a psychological assessment.

SOLE RESIDENTS

Lester and Val Cain are the sole residents of Middleton, Queensland, Australia, where they run the historic Middleton Hotel—the only occupied building in the area. They are nearly 106 mi (170 km) from the nearest town but have run the hotel for more than 15 years.

SAME NAME

The easternmost and westernmost points of the territorial United States (located in the U.S. Virgin Islands and Guam, respectively) are both called Point Udall. They are named in honor of politician brothers Stewart and Morris Udall.

CLIFF CRUISE

The Sun Cruise Resort in Jeongdongjin, South Korea, looks like a cruise ship that has run aground on top of a cliff!

The cruise is more than 500 ft (152 m) long, about 150 ft (45 m) tall, and has 211 rooms. Much like an actual vessel, the hotel offers guests a multitude of entertainment options, like shopping, karaoke, swimming pools, and volleyball courts—all without the rocking waves that can cause seasickness. There is also a sailboat-shaped sushi restaurant just a short walk down the beach! Sounds of waves lapping the side of the faux cruise liner are pumped out from speakers to further imitate the experience of being out on the ocean.

TATTOO SHADES

As she is highly sensitive to light, Mandy Liscombe, from Swansea, Wales, has had ink tattooed onto her eyeballs to act as sunglasses. Surgeon Mario Saldanha inserted tattoo ink into Liscombe's corneas to filter the light, effectively creating a pair of shades inside her eyes.

HARMONICA PRANK

For a prank, Ontario high school student Mollie O'Brien stuffed an entire harmonica inside her mouth, filling it from cheek to cheek—but the instrument became stuck there and she had to go to the hospital to have it removed. Whenever she breathed, it made a musical noise.

PLAYED VIOLIN

Dagmar Turner, from the Isle of Wight, England, played the violin while surgeons operated on her brain to remove a tumor. They asked Turner to play so they could ensure that the parts of the brain which control hand movements and coordination were not damaged during the procedure.

SHARP REMINDER

Mr. Chen, from Changsha, China, lived for 10 years unaware that he had eight embroidery needles stuck in his right buttock. He often felt a stinging sensation there, and when he finally went to the doctor, an X-ray revealed the sharp needles. He then recalled that he had once fallen into a pile of trash at work (which included metal needles), but thought that he had removed them all.

HEADLESS TORSO

DNA was used in 2019 to identify the body of a man who had been last seen alive more than 100 years earlier. Convicted murderer Joseph Loveless escaped from jail in 1916, and a headless torso was found wrapped in a sack in an Idaho cave in 1979. Forty years later, the body was revealed to be that of Loveless. Scientists confirmed the identity via 2,000 hours of research by comparing the body's DNA to that of Loveless's living grandson.

SKELETON PASSENGER

Police in Tempe, Arizona, pulled over a driver for using a carpool lane when his only passenger was a skeleton wearing a hat. The skeleton, who was also wearing bandages, was sitting propped up in the passenger seat.

HORROR WEDDING

Detroit residents Jeff Peabody and his wife Alexis dressed as Frankenstein and his bride at their horror-themed wedding on Halloween, which was attended by 180 guests in costume. Bridesmaids were the Creature from the Black Lagoon and a mummy, while the two best men were dressed as Dracula and Wolfman. The seating plan was arranged to resemble a cemetery.

IN TREBLE

If you're feeling musical, take a walk down Tianma Pier in Yantai, China! The twists and turns create the familiar shape of a treble clef, used in musical notation to indicate the pitch of notes on a staff.

FAN FEED

SHIVER ME TIMBERS!

This swashbuckling speed machine was submitted to us by Bill and Kelly Rigoni, owners of Northern Exposure Gallery in Port Clinton, Ohio. The couple spent a year constructing a 32-ft-tall (9.8-m) pirate ship on wheels, complete with a mast, rigging, and sails, and dubbed it the Northern Exposure Landship. To create their one-of-a-kind "ARRRVEE," they bought a Coachmen RV from the now-closed College Football Hall of Fame in South Bend, Indiana. Then, they dedicated nine months to outfitting the interior with nautical décor, transforming it into a traveling storefront.

CLEARLY BETTER

VACANT

Transparent public restrooms are a game changer in Japan, despite their counterintuitive designs.

Public toilets tend to get a bad rap—and for good reason. While Japan boasts some of the world's cleanest facilities, many people remain hesitant to use them. Some fear dirty interiors, while others have concerns about people lying in wait inside. To address these concerns, Japan tasked its most innovative architects with renovating 17 facilities in Shibuya's public parks, two of which ended up with this inventive redesign. Capable of being inspected from the outside, officials hope these clear units will inspire public confidence. Oh, and don't worry, the glass turns opaque once the door is locked, meaning you can do your business in private.

OCCUPIED

FEEL THE BURN

Ivan Djuric of Uzice, Serbia, creates hyper-realistic portraits using a technique known as *pyrography*, which involves burning different shading values into wood.

With a pen-like wood burning tool, Djuric uses varying and precise amounts of pressure to change the intensity of the burn. Using this method, he is able to achieve an astonishing amount of detail, with his finished products resembling black-and-white photographs. Subjects of his blazing artistry have included Chadwick Boseman, Luciano Pavarotti, Jerry Garcia, Dwayne "The Rock" Johnson, and Snoop Dogg.

Actor Dwayne "The Rock" Johnson.

Acclaimed Italian opera singer Luciano Pavarotti.

Jerry Garcia, lead guitarist and vocalist of the Grateful Dead.

Actor Chadwick Boseman.

CHECK IT OUT

In 2017, International Space Station astronauts released images from northern Idaho's Whitetail Butte. The photos show a near-perfect checkerboard, the result of nineteenth-century forest-management techniques. These techniques required the reservation of alternating 1-sq-mi (2.6-sq-m) parcels of land. The lighter squares are filled with small, young trees that reveal the snow on the ground. The darker ones are parcels of thick, intact forest, where the snow is not visible from a bird's-eye view.

THANKS A BUNCH

Believe it or not, the yellow grocery store banana you know and love didn't always look that way! Before humans began cultivating the fruit thousands of years ago, bananas were much smaller and had large seeds. The most popular variety is the Cavendish, which are all genetically identical to the seedless plant propagated by British Duke William Cavendish in 1834. There are still hundreds of other varieties found around the world, including some with large, hard seeds, like the Cavendish's ancestor.

PORCELAIN PROFIT

Judith Howard purchased an eighteenth-century French porcelain dish for $17 at a thrift store in Berkshire, England, in 1982, and in 2020 it sold at auction for about $32,000—a profit of nearly 2,000 percent.

LOTTERY WIN

Natalia Escudero, a reporter for Spanish TV station RTVE, quit her job live on air while giving a report on a lottery drawing in December 2019 when she realized that she was one of the winners. However, she later learned she had only won around $5,500.

TRICKY PROBLEM

After inventing the Rubik's Cube, it took Hungarian architecture professor Erno Rubik about a month to solve it.

SURPRISE CONNECTION

New York couple Stephen Lee and Helen Jacoby were looking through old family photos while celebrating their engagement when they realized that her mother and his late father had themselves nearly got married in Korea in the 1960s before going their separate ways. Until then, they had no idea there was any previous connection between their two families.

COLOR BLIND

When he retired, Emerson Moser, the senior crayon maker at Crayola, admitted he was color blind. He molded 1.4 billion crayons during his 35-year career with the company.

HUGE HAIRBALL

Doctors in Kolomna, Russia, removed a giant hairball from a 30-year-old woman's ovaries with strands up to 5-in-long (12.5-cm)! The cyst was causing her abdominal pain and had likely been growing inside her since birth.

SECRET MESSAGE

In November 2019, workers carrying out renovations at Montclair State University's College Hall in New Jersey discovered a 112-year-old message in a bottle tucked into a secret compartment inside a wall. Dated July 3, 1907, the message was written and signed by William Hanley and James Lennon, the two Newark bricklayers who built the original wall.

JELLY BEANS

Ronald Reagan had 3.5 tons of red, white, and blue jelly beans shipped to Washington, D.C., for his presidential inauguration. Afterward, he placed a standing order for 720 bags of jelly beans per month.

RESCUE FLUKE

When a train careened over the end of elevated tracks in the Netherlands in November 2020, an unlikely hero helped prevent a disaster: a massive statue of a whale's tail!

Onlookers reported the train derailment looked like a scene from a Hollywood movie. Noted was the presence of the statue, which prevented the train from a steep plummet. Fortunately, the train only had one passenger during the incident, the driver Mr. Natrop. He was taken to the hospital for evaluation and later questioned at the police station. Officials have since investigated how the safety systems designed to prevent derailment failed.

KEYSTONE CURIOS

The globetrotting Robert Ripley brought home artifacts from his journeys, which today form the heart of the greatest collection of oddities ever assembled—found only at Ripley's Believe It or Not! Odditoriums around the world.

While the current Ripley's collection spans everything from pop culture items to collections of belly button lint, the exhibits hand-selected by Ripley himself truly carry on his legacy. Shrunken heads, Tibetan kapalas, Fiji mermaids, and more—these curios have become the keystones of Ripley's Believe It or Not!

Shrunken Heads

Robert Ripley learned about shrunken heads, or *tsantas*, in his 1925 trip to South America, where he purchased one in Panama for $100. Created by members of the Jivaro tribes of Ecuador and Peru, the process of creating a shrunken head is long and complicated, consisting of removing the skull, boiling the scalp, and filling the insides with hot rocks and sand before it is reshaped and sewn shut. There are more than 100 genuine shrunken heads in the Ripley's collection.

To:
TED STONE
—ALL THE BEST!
from
RIPLEY ———
and
HIS SEEING-EYE DOG
"CYCLOPS"
BELIEVE IT or NOT

Pranks of Nature

Cows with six legs, lambs with two faces—
these are what Robert Ripley called "pranks
of nature." Looking like the work of a twisted
taxidermist but 100% natural, the creatures in the
Ripley's collection include (but aren't limited to)
conjoined piglets, a sheep with two heads, and
goats with one eye. Ripley himself joked about
owning a one-eyed dog named Cyclops, which was
actually his sheepdog with his long hair cleverly
combed to cover one eye.

Tibetan Kapala

A "kapala" is a bowl used by Tibetan Buddhists and Indian Hindus in rituals—and they're made from the skulls of monks. There are two types of kapala—those that use the whole skull and those that use only the skull cap or the top half of the cranium. They often serve as vessels for holding food or wine.

Fiji Mermaid

One of the most famous sideshow artifacts of all time. Originally presented as an authentic specimen by showmen such as P. T. Barnum, the mermaids were later revealed to be fakes, or "gaffs," constructed of monkey and fish parts taxidermied together. Ripley never portrayed the Fiji mermaids in his collection as real, preferring to highlight the craftsmanship instead.

Masakichi Statue

One of Ripley's most prized possessions—a wooden, life-sized self-portrait by Japanese artist Hananuma Masakichi, completed in the 1880s. The piece is said to have been started by Masakichi after he was diagnosed with tuberculosis, and was intended as a gift for his wife. He was incredibly precise, even plucking his own hair from his head and inserting it into thousands of tiny holes in the wood, like real hair follicles. Robert Ripley bought the statue from a San Francisco antiques shop in 1934.

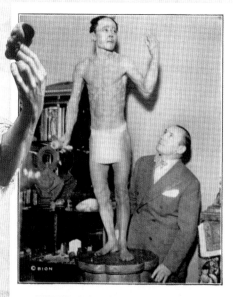

THE JAPANESE MAN

THIS Oriental image is so realistic in detail that it seems the man himself stands there in flesh and blood. And such was the artist's intention! It was carved by Hananuma Masakichi, the illustrious Japanese artist, as a reproduction of himself.

Mr. Ripley avers this is the most lifelike image ever made by man. He searched the world over for this statue for 20 years and finally found it in a small Oriental curio shop.

Over 2,000 pieces of wood were used in it. The body is made of hundreds of pieces or strips glued together—no nails, screws or metals were used. Made in Yokohama in 1885, it shows the artist at the age of 53. Hananuma, suffering from tuberculosis, realized that his end was near and sought to leave a monument of himself. The result is undoubtedly the greatest work of art of its kind ever done.

An exact counterpart of the artist, the size is the same, the pose, the features, the skin is the same color and apparent texture, the hair is the same, the blue veins, the muscles, the prominent collarbones, the tubercular hollows in the neck, the outlines of the ribs, even the hairs adorning the figure. Each separate hair was plucked from his own body and inserted—one by one—in holes bored for them. He took out his own teeth and put them inside the mouth. He removed his own finger-nails and toe-nails and fixed them on the figure. The eyes were made of glass by Hananuma himself and are a wonder of the optical profession, so human and alive are they. Finally, Masakichi added his own carving tools, loin cloth and spectacles, and in his will left all of his worldly goods to his image.

Strange and fascinating, this figure symbolizes the curious facts assembled by Robert L. Ripley of "Believe It or Not" fame which we are bringing to you the coming twelve months. This folder is the first, the other eleven following at monthly intervals.

Please accept them with our compliments and let them be a reminder of our desire to be of service.

RIPLEY BELIEVE IT OR NOT, INC., NEW YORK, N. Y.

Blind Bust

Mark Shoesmith of New York sculpted this bust of Robert Ripley in 1938. Remarkably, Shoesmith was blind and achieved Ripley's likeness purely by touching his face. By the age of 36, Shoesmith's hands were so damaged from creating his art that he had to give up reading Braille for pleasure.

Devil and Damsel Statue

Around 1928, Robert Ripley acquired a truly remarkable artifact while visiting Germany—a double-sided, solid fruitwood statue that depicts the devil on one side and a fair damsel on the other. The life-size statue was crafted so skillfully that you cannot see one while facing the other.

Side view

Damsel

Devil

THE ARSENIC WALTZ.

THE NEW DANCE OF DEATH. (DEDICATED TO THE GREEN WREATH AND DRESS-MONGERS.)

FATAL FASHION

Upon reaching a certain age, looking back at your clothing choices from your younger years can make you feel like dying of embarrassment, but over the years, there have been fashion trends that could quite literally kill you. These are some of history's deadliest getups.

1 Scheele's Green

Invented in 1775 by Swedish chemist Carl Wilhelm Scheele, this strikingly emerald shade was poisonous, thanks to the arsenic used to create it. It was used to dye fabric, causing rashes and oozing sores on those who wore it. But it was the factory workers handling the pigment all day long who suffered the severest side effects, including death.

2 Time's Up

During World War I, women began working factory jobs—one of which involved painting glowing radium onto watch faces so they could be read in the dark. The then-unknown effects of radium poisoning eventually caused dozens of women's deaths, many of which were preceded by rotting teeth, brittle bones, and large tumors.

3 Burning Ballet Dancers

Ballet dancers put their bodies through intense training in order to pull off their signature moves, but in the nineteenth century, there was an even bigger threat to their well-being. Thanks to a combination of long, fluffy, flammable skirts and gas lamps that lined the stage, there were multiple instances of dancers catching on fire and perishing from the ensuing blaze.

4 Stiff Neck

Around the end of the nineteenth century, it was fashionable for Western men to wear high, stiff collars. There were multiple instances in which men died from the collars cutting off their circulation, earning the accessories the nickname of "father killers."

WAX ON, WAX OFF

The central part of the Pysanka Museum in Kolomyia, Ukraine, is built in the shape of a giant, 46-ft-tall (14-m) painted egg.

The museum houses a collection of more than 10,000 decorated Ukrainian Easter eggs, or "pysanky," some dating back over a century! The art form itself has existed for even longer. To create a pysanka, an artist heats a pencil-like tool filled with wax to draw a design onto the egg. Once the wax is dried, the egg is dipped in dye, removed, and further designs are added, with the process repeating until the artist is finished and all of the wax is melted off the egg. The decorated eggs are preserved by blowing the inside of the egg out through a small hole.

300 HORSEPOWER ENGINE!

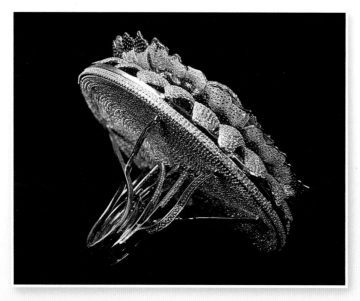

RING BLING

Indian jewelry designer Harshit Bansal created a ring with 12,638 natural diamonds! He accomplished this feat by designing the "Ring of Prosperity" with layers like the petals of a flower, specifically a marigold—a symbol of luck in India. The eye-catching jewelry weighs 5.8 oz (165 g), slightly more than a baseball!

INCREDI-BIKE

The one-of-a-kind TMC Dumont motorcycle is powered by an airplane engine!

Created by retired Formula One driver Tarso Marques of Brazil, the futuristic vehicle also boasts massive 36-in (91-cm) hubless wheels that are almost tall enough to block the rider's view. The engine was lifted from a 1960s aircraft and had to be taken apart, cleaned, and reassembled from the ground up in order to safely supply the bike with 300 horsepower! The TMC Dumont was built completely in Brazil, a matter of pride for Marques, over the course of 15 years and won "Best of Show" at the 2018 Daytona Bike Week.

FATAL WAGER

Subhash Yadav died while trying to eat 50 eggs in a single sitting as part of a $28 wager with a friend in Uttar Pradesh, India. When the two men argued, Yadav accepted the egg-eating challenge but collapsed after devouring 41 and died a few hours later in the hospital from overeating.

LOCKED DOOR

A 19-year-old man was soon arrested after robbing a Pizza Hut in Las Cruces, New Mexico, because he accidentally face-planted into a locked door and left behind incriminating DNA evidence.

FRAGILE EARL

John Bligh, the third Earl of Darnley, who served as a member of parliament in Ireland in the eighteenth century, was convinced that he was a fine China teapot and feared that his spout would fall off during the night.

MEET SATAN

A spelling mistake in a newspaper ad for a Christmas fair in Courtenay, British Columbia, Canada, accidentally invited people to take photos with Satan!

SAME CARD

Best friends Alan Braithwaite and Chris Oakley, from Worcestershire, England, have been sending the same Christmas card back and forth to each other for more than 50 years. There is no longer much space on the card to write a message.

SUPPORT CLOWN

Fearing that he might lose his job at a New Zealand advertising agency, Joshua Jack took an emotional support clown to an important work meeting. He hired Joe the Clown for $200 in an attempt to lighten the mood with his employers. In the end, he was still fired, but he did have two balloon animals—a unicorn and a poodle—that the clown had made noisily during the meeting.

SAUSAGE SALES

Volkswagen sells more sausages than cars. In 2019, the company produced 6.2 million cars at its factories across the world, but at its Wolfsburg, Germany, plant, it made 6.8 million currywurst sausages, which sell in more than a dozen countries.

In 2019, a fugitive was arrested after being found asleep on a bed in an IKEA in Uppsala, Sweden. The man had stayed in the furniture store after it closed.

LIVING GOD

Six-year-old Shivam Kumar, who lives in a village near Delhi, India, was born with an unusually long patch of hair on his lower back that looks like a tail, leading neighbors to believe he is a reincarnation of the Hindu monkey god Hanuman. Villagers showered him with so many gifts that his parents were forced to hide him away from the unwanted attention.

SEA SQUIRM

Believe it or not, this flowing, tube-like object is actually a colony of thousands of creatures! Two divers were filming a tourism video off the coast of a New Zealand island when they came across the 26-ft-long (8-m) pyrosome, which is made up of tiny, individual organisms called *zooids*. Together, they swim to the ocean's surface at night to feed on microscopic plankton and then return to the depths before daytime.

DUCK DIET

Veterinarians at an animal hospital in Pattaya, Thailand, removed 32 rubber ducks from the stomach of Devil the American bulldog. He had broken into a box of 50 yellow toy ducks, which had been bought by his owner Nong Aom to decorate a swimming pool, and had eaten 38 of them. He vomited up six chewed ducks before Nong took him to the hospital.

MULTIPLE BIRTHS

Mary Jane, a Great Dane and American bulldog mix owned by Joanne Hine from the Isle of Man, gave birth naturally to a litter of 21 puppies.

SUPER POOPER

A blue whale can eject up to 44 gal (200 l) of poop in a single bowel movement.

HORSE PASSENGER

A horse found running loose among traffic in Cardiff, Wales, was captured by passersby and loaded onto a city bus. The bus driver lent his vehicle as transport when police officers said it would take time to get a horse trailer to the scene. The horse was then taken on a five-minute ride on the bus to be reunited with its owners in a parking lot.

BAGGY IS BEAUTIFUL

The Titicaca water frog of South America is covered in wrinkly skin! This feature helps the fully aquatic amphibian absorb oxygen from the frigid and high-altitude waters of Lake Titicaca, located between Bolivia and Peru. The unique species has even been observed doing underwater "push-ups" as a way to get more water, and therefore extra oxygen, between the folds of its wrinkles! Sadly, Titicaca water frog populations are shrinking at an alarming rate, partially due to destruction of their natural habitat.

BIG GULP

A humpback whale got more than it bargained for when it accidentally scooped up a sea lion while feeding in Monterey Bay, California.

Fortunately for the sea lion, humpback whales are filter feeders and have no interest in eating anything larger than a few inches long. The photographer who captured this moment, Chase Dekker, confirmed that the sea lion made it out of the whale's mouth.

A humpback whale can grow larger than a school bus, yet its esophagus is only about the same width as a small melon.

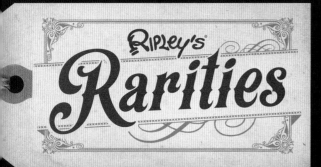

Ripley's Rarities

Ripley's Exhibit
Cat. No. 175119

ATHENS OLYMPIC MEDAL

Bronze medal from the first modern Olympic Games, which were held in Athens, Greece, in 1896 in homage to their ancient beginnings. The front features Zeus holding Nike, the goddess of victory.

Ripley's Exhibit
Cat. No. 2359

OLYMPIC PRESS PASS

Robert Ripley's press pass to the 1928 Olympics in Amsterdam, The Netherlands. Before starting the *Believe It or Not!* cartoon, Ripley was a sports cartoonist.

Ripley's Exhibit
Cat. No. 173020

SIGNED OLYMPIC TORCH

An Olympic torch from the 1960 Games held in Rome, Italy. Signed by legendary boxer Muhammad Ali, who went on to win the gold medal in boxing, light heavyweight division, that same year.

MUHAMMAD ALI

Believe It or Not! BIO

It's no hidden feat that Muhammad Ali tops the charts as one of the world's most renowned and talented boxers.

Over the course of two decades, he won 56 fights and lost only five. He also spouted one of the most iconic quotes in the history of sports: "Float like a butterfly, sting like a bee." And while much is known about the boxing legend, there are some things that may surprise you!

Bicycle Blues
Muhammad Ali, born Cassius Marcellus Clay Jr., grew up in Louisville, Kentucky. When he was 12 years old, someone stole his red Schwinn bicycle. Clay reported the theft to local police officer Joe E. Martin.

Clay was so angry about the incident that he swore to "whup" whoever took his bike. And while those were fighting words, Clay had no actual fighting experience. Officer Martin, who also happened to be a boxing trainer, suggested that Clay learn how to properly box before he confronted the thief. He took Martin up on his offer and a few weeks later won his first fight in a split decision.

Missing Medal
In 1960, the USA boxing team selected Ali for the Rome Olympics. The 18-year-old boxer was afraid to fly, but his trainer, Joe Martin, convinced him to go after reasoning that the only way to become a heavyweight champion was to take part in the Olympics. Ali competed in the light heavyweight division and emerged victorious over the more experienced Zigzy Pietrzykowski, landing a gold medal in the process.

Believe it or not, no one knows where Ali's original gold medal is. Urban legend says he threw it into the Ohio River after being turned away from a restaurant for being Black, but Ali has never confirmed this story, even saying, "I never knew what I done with that medal." All in all, things ended up all right. He received a replacement medal during the 1996 Atlanta Olympics, where he also lit the Olympic Flame.

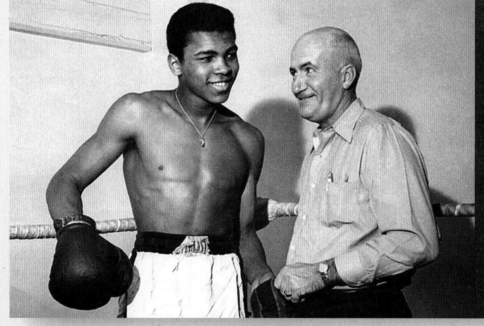

Musical Muhammad

During his time away from boxing, Ali focused his energies on a totally different career: acting and singing! He appeared in the 1969 Broadway production *Buck White*, in New York City. Ali was friends with actor-producer Ron Rich and often spent time with the cast backstage. When he showed off his singing ability, producer Zev Buffman was quite impressed and decided to put Ali in the show and turn it into a musical.

"I was amazed at his ability to carry a tune—his voice was as attention-grabbing as his charm as a fighter," Bufman told the New York Times in 2019. Unfortunately, the show didn't resonate with audiences, and it shut down just four days after its debut. It's unclear why it failed, but it is an interesting footnote to Ali's career.

Big Book

In 2003, German art book publisher Taschen released 10,000 copies of *GOAT: A Tribute to Muhammad Ali*. The book contains 3,000 images and 600,000 words. It also weighs 75 pounds, and the first 1,000 signed copies went on sale for $7,500.

The Champ's Edition of the book costs a little more—around $15,000. However, these deluxe books are sold with a sculpture by Jeff Koons and are signed by both the artist and Ali himself. Today, you can get the original book at a deep discount of $6,000 from the publisher.

TASCHEN

EARLY START

Jay-Z's daughter Blue Ivy was featured on his song "Glory" when she was only two days old. The song opens with her first heartbeat and includes a sample of her cries at the end.

SCOOBY SWITCH

Instead of a Great Dane, Scooby-Doo was originally going to be a sheepdog called Too Much. The name of Scooby-Doo was taken from Frank Sinatra's scat line in the song "Strangers in the Night."

TYPED ARTWORKS

James Cook, from Essex, England, creates portraits and landscapes using the keys of five old typewriters, some dating back to the 1950s. It can take him up to 30 hours to type out a drawing of a celebrity like former *Doctor Who* actor Tom Baker or Tom Hanks, always starting with the eyes (which are the most difficult). He uses the typewriter's @ symbol for shading because it has the largest surface area.

When U.S. rapper Cardi B mentioned her dentist in the song "Bodak Yellow," fans tracked down Dr. Catrise Austin and her New York City business tripled.

COFFEE PORTRAITS

Spanish artist Nuria Salcedo creates amazing portraits of Hollywood celebrities such as Eddie Redmayne and Jared Leto by painting with coffee. She started out drawing with traditional pencils but found coffee to be a much better medium. To achieve different shades of brown in her artwork, she adds several layers of coffee.

ONE-ARMED DRUMMER

Rick Allen continues to play drums with the rock band Def Leppard even though his left arm was amputated in 1985.

NO LAUGHING MATTER

A hyena researcher sued Disney for "defamation of character" for its portrayal of the animals as villains in *The Lion King*.

SOUND EFFECTS

Sound designer and voice actor Ben Burtt created a library of 2,400 different sounds for the title robot in *WALL-E*. They included Burtt sneezing while a vacuum cleaner was running (for WALL-E sneezing), a camera shutter (for WALL-E's eyebrow movements), and the sound of cars being wrecked at a demolition derby (for WALL-E compressing trash).

MUSICAL ANVILS

Richard Wagner's *Das Rheingold* has musical parts for 18 metal anvils—nine small, six medium, and three large—tuned to three octaves apart.

HAY, THERE!

Beth Bays of Huddleston, Virginia, paid homage to legendary country singer Willie Nelson with a 15-ft-tall (4.5-m) sculpture assembled from hay. Complete with Nelson's signature pigtails and guitar, she named the piece "Will-Hay Nelson." Bays has completed other hay masterpieces over the years, including figures inspired by *The Wizard of Oz* and Virginia Tech's mascot, the HokieBird.

WILL-HAY NELSON

ALIEN APARTMENT

A nondescript city apartment in Barcelona, Spain, houses sci-fi fan Luis Nostromo's extraterrestrial treasure trove, an homage to Ridley Scott.

The 43-year-old *Alien* enthusiast has gone to incredible lengths to honor the classic films, recreating portions of Ash's laboratory, situated in the auxiliary ship *Narcissus*. He has also remade the hallway where the Marines and Ripley discovered Newt in *Aliens*, part of the Hadley's Hope complex. Besides reconstructing spaceships from Scott's franchise, Nostromo also boasts an impressive collection of original and replica props, further enhancing his chest-popping home décor.

STONE HOME

Caddisfly larvae living in creeks have developed an ingenious way to avoid predators and being swept downstream. They encase themselves in tiny stone structures held together by sticky strips of silk emitted from their bodies. Inspired by this incredible adaptation, French artist Hubert Duprat has utilized the insects since the early 1980s to craft jewelry. Instead of gravel, he provides the larvae with precious metals, pearls, and gemstones, allowing the artistic process to run its course.

The insects can build with almost any material, as evidenced by these gold and pearl creations.

ENDEMIC ANIMALS

Around 100 different animal species can be found nowhere else in the world except the island of Borneo, including proboscis monkeys, Bornean clouded leopards, Bornean orangutans, and Bornean pygmy elephants.

CAT LADDERS

Residents of many Swiss towns and cities have erected a network of custom-built ladders and ramps on the sides of multi-story apartment blocks so that their cats can move around freely outdoors.

MUSICAL APE

Tal, a music-loving orangutan at Chahinkapa Zoo, in Wahpeton, North Dakota, has played the recorder with a classical music ensemble, the New York Kammermusiker. Tal blows into the recorder while zookeeper Addy Paul operates the instrument's valves.

ESCAPE ARTIST

Quilty, a cat at a rescue shelter in Houston, Texas, is so skilled at opening doors that the center had to install new security measures to stop him from freeing the other cats.

TINY PUP

At six and a half months old, Tweety "Piolin," a Chihuahua puppy owned by Vanesa Semler of Kissimmee, Florida, weighed just 6 oz (170 g) and was only 2.6 in (6.5 cm) tall and 2.4 in (6 cm) long.

GIANT PARROT

Heracles inexpectatus, a species of parrot that lived in New Zealand 19 million years ago, weighed over 15 lb (7 kg) and stood 3.3 ft (1 m) tall—more than half the average height of a human.

MOSS BOSS

The Vietnamese mossy frog's three-dimensional camouflage is the animal kingdom's version of a ghillie suit. Coupled with its ability to throw its voice like a ventriloquist, few amphibians have better mastered the art of disguise. Researchers report the frog can produce calls that sound like they originated up to 13 ft (4 m) away from where it actually is. Making them almost impossible to find in the wild. And when these moving piles of greenery get scared? They roll up and play dead, further perplexing potential predators.

RISKY RELOCATION

Hundreds of mountain goats took to the skies over Olympic National Park, part of a massive relocation project to prevent them from harassing hikers for their salty sweat and pee!

The goats became a nuisance when their cravings for salt and minerals led them to campsites to lick up cooking wastewater, as well as human urine and sweat. Helicopter crews flew over remote areas, tranquilized the agile animals from the air, and then bagged the non-native creatures, whisking them to reception points. There, biologists handled relocation preparations. Since mountain goats weigh up to 300 lb (136 kg), the operation proved dicey at times. Nonetheless, hundreds of billies made their way to the North Cascades, their native environment, where natural salt licks are plentiful, nixing the need to harass unwitting humans.

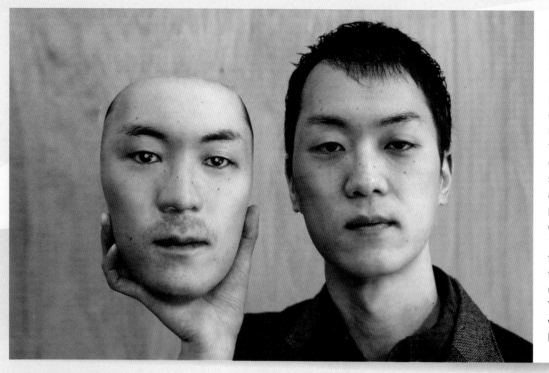

FACE OFF

Shuhei Okawara's "That Face" project relies on photos and 3D data to create handmade masks so realistic you'll do a double-take. He sells the uncanny creations at his Tokyo store Kamenya Omote and online, where you can purchase a mask for upward of 98,000 yen. More than 100 people submitted their faces for mask-ification to Okawara, who ended up choosing the face of a Tokyo man in his thirties, with plans to add more to his lifelike lineup.

MUPPET STAR

The first nationally famous Muppet was not Kermit the Frog but Rowlf the Dog! Rowlf joined *The Jimmy Dean Show* in 1963 and was soon receiving more than 2,000 fan letters a week—more than Dean himself.

CREEPY DOLL

Woody in *Toy Story* was originally intended to be a talking ventriloquist's doll, but film company executives decided that would be too creepy and changed the character to a talking cowboy doll.

COFFEE CANTATA

German composer Johann Sebastian Bach wrote a mini opera, *Schweigt stille, plaudert nicht* ("Be still, stop chattering"), about coffee addiction. Bach himself was addicted to coffee and drank up to 30 cups a day.

PAPER SCULPTURE

Students at the Indiana University South Bend Fine Arts Club created a 14-ft-tall (4.3-m) papier-mâché sculpture made from old Martin's Super Markets comment cards and 60 gal (273 l) of wheat paste.

BAND CAMEO

No Doubt made a background cameo appearance in *The Simpsons* episode "Homerpalooza," thanks to a family connection. Gwen Stefani's older brother Eric was an animator on the show at the time, so he added the band to the scene.

ICONIC OUTFIT

The iconic black leather jacket and pants worn by Olivia Newton-John in the 1978 movie *Grease* sold for more than $500,000 at auction in Los Angeles in 2019.

HEART OF STONE

On the border between Brazil and Uruguay, miners for Uruguay Minerals unearthed a stunning, heart-shaped geode. Several miners were struggling to excavate a new mineral vein when they broke open a large rock, revealing the one-of-a-kind geological feature that would make Cupid blush.

MOUTH MUSIC

Swedish builder Love Hultén created a surreal music-making machine out of 25 plastic chattering teeth!

With each push of a key on the VOC-25, as it is called, a corresponding mouth opens wide and sings a digital note. By turning the dials on the console, Hultén can alter the sound of the voices, ranging from an angelic choir to demonic screaming—all of which are accompanied by the clacking of the teeth opening and closing. Believe it or not, Hultén is not the first person to build something like this. He took his inspiration from inventor Simone Giertz, who built a similar machine based on the novel idea that large groups of people could clack their teeth together as an alternative to clapping.

BUTTERFLY EFFECT

With a delicate hand, artist Fiona Parkinson removes shapes from butterfly wings and rearranges them to create a stunning series of artworks titled *Insect Dissectology*.

Parkinson's work combines traditional taxidermy and preservation methods with modern techniques and tools to craft her pieces. She cuts the wings of butterfly specimens into fragile shapes and patterns, creating whimsical homages to nature, life, and death. To realize her hyper-precise designs, she uses a unique preservation technique. While she won't reveal the exact details of this innovation, Parkinson did sit down with Ripley's to satisfy some of our other curiosities.

Terribly Beautiful features one of Parkinson's favorite butterflies, the giant blue morpho, as well as one of her fears—a tarantula!

Q: What is *Insect Dissectology*, and what does it mean to you?

A: A "dissectologist" is someone who enjoys doing and solving puzzles. The themes of my work itself are very personal, having to do with my own experiences. I found that creating something puzzle-like allowed me to express the journey I was on to find myself and solve the puzzle of my life. More so, I learned that using real specimens added emotional value to the work I was producing, and since much of my work has its origins in science labs in a university setting, *Insect Dissectology* was born!

Q: How do you source your insects?

A: Taxidermists get their specimens from all over the place, but almost all of my specimens are acquired from conservation projects established to help protect natural populations. Allowing local people to breed species endemic to where they live provides them with a source of income while also reducing poaching and the destruction of the natural environment.

Q: Does your preservation process make the insects easier to work with, or are they as delicate as they appear?
A: Butterflies and moths are *very* fragile; in fact, it's almost impossible to touch them without causing damage!

As I was developing *Dissectology*, this wasn't a concern to me, as I was making the pieces for myself. Now that I'm fortunate enough to be sending some of my work around the world, I have had to develop techniques to make them sturdier. It is very important to me, however, that they keep a sense of fragility, as this is an important feature of the art.

Q: How are your pieces mounted and displayed?
A: The mounting is challenging, although it really only involves glue and pins. I arrange the pins in foam board and then carefully glue the tiny pieces of wings on top, using very gentle fingers and tweezers, all while holding my breath!

Q: What are your favorite butterfly and moth species?
A: I think I would have to say that my favorite butterfly is the blue morpho, specifically the *Morpho menelaus zischkai*. Their color is just stunning, and their structure is so complex that scientists are studying them to develop holograms that can't be counterfeited.

In terms of moths, I have to go with the death's-head hawkmoth. They were made famous (and scary!) by *The Silence of the Lambs*, but actually they're really cute, fluffy creatures when you look at them up-close!

A REAL MOTH!

Weathervein is made up of two different morpho butterfly species: the luna morpho and the blue morpho.

NGC 6302 is named after the Butterfly Nebula and was created using the aptly named comet moth.

Q: What is something surprising you have learned while working on this series?

A: When you're working with the specimens that I am, it is hard not to be surprised by their beauty and diversity every day, and I discover new things about them so often! Only recently, I looked at them for the first time under microscope cameras and realized that on some of the butterflies I use, the blue is made from tiny scales while the black is made from hairs!

Oh... and I'm still scared of spiders and have nightmares about them (butterflies, too) coming to life!

Memento Mori, made with a flying handkerchief butterfly and death's-head hawkmoth. The phrase "memento mori" is a Latin phrase meaning "remember that you have to die."

"Butterflies and moths are very fragile; in fact, it's almost impossible to touch them without causing damage!"

Metamorphosis, created using the nearly all-black giant swallowtail butterfly.

1 Bladen Pietro

Bladen Pietro is a YouTuber whose channel focuses on gaming and traveling. He was born with osteogenesis imperfecta, or "brittle bone disease," and has broken more than 200 bones in his body. But Pietro, known as Bastrin online, lives life without fear and is an inspiration to his nearly 600,000 subscribers.

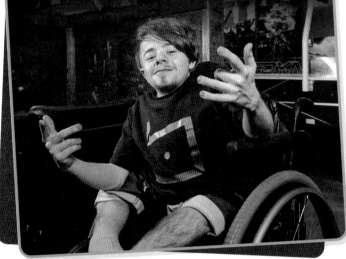

POSITIVE INFLUENCE

The world of social media has created an unprecedented opportunity for people of all walks of life to interact with each other.

Here are just a few of the many internet personalities who use their platforms to make a positive difference.

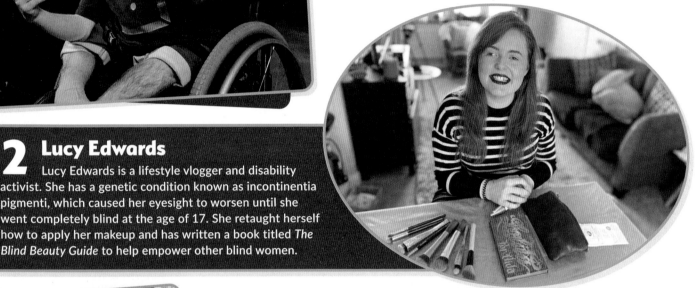

2 Lucy Edwards

Lucy Edwards is a lifestyle vlogger and disability activist. She has a genetic condition known as incontinentia pigmenti, which caused her eyesight to worsen until she went completely blind at the age of 17. She retaught herself how to apply her makeup and has written a book titled *The Blind Beauty Guide* to help empower other blind women.

4 Hajra Khan

Hajra Khan is captain of the Pakistani Women's National Soccer Team. On Twitter, she advocates for women in sports and vocalizes the challenges of being a female athlete, as well as promoting the importance of mental health care.

3 Helena Gualinga

Helena Gualinga is a 17-year-old indigenous rights and climate change activist who grew up in the Ecuadorian Amazon. On her Instagram account, she shares stories about her community and posts photos showing how the Amazon rainforest is being negatively affected by climate change.

5 Theland Kicknosway

Theland Kicknosway, a.k.a. @the_land, uses his platform on TikTok to shed light on indigenous culture and issues in North America. He is Wolf Clan, of the Potawatami and Cree Nation, and a member of Walpole Island, Bkejwanong Territory, in Southern Ontario. For the past seven years, he has helped organize a fundraising marathon to raise awareness about Missing and Murdered Indigenous Women and Girls (MMIWG).

GREATER THAN

Clark is also a motivational speaker. He encourages people to be "greater than" their obstacles.

Zion Clark of Massillon, Ohio, is on a mission to become the first athlete to win a medal at both the Olympics and Paralympics in the same year!

Clark was born without legs due to caudal regression syndrome, a rare condition that affects about 1 in 100,000 newborns. He faced uncertainty and bullying during his childhood, but made a place for himself in the world of wrestling. In high school, Clark competed against able-bodied wrestlers and nearly qualified for the Ohio State Wrestling Championships! He also participated in wheelchair races at the state level. Now he attends Kent State, where he is on the wrestling team, and is training to participate in both the Olympics (as a wrestler) and the Paralympics (as a wheelchair racer).

MATCHMAKERS

THE "FINGERPRINT FACTORY" INSIDE THE D.C. ARMORY

In addition to its Most Wanted list, the FBI has plenty of files on celebrities. People such as Lucille Ball, Truman Capote, and Marilyn Monroe each have a file.

DINER ARTIFACTS
Richard Gutman, of Allentown, Pennsylvania, spent 48 years collecting artifacts relating to American diners—including menus, matchboxes, toothpicks, postcards, and more than 7,000 photographs.

WHEELIE RIDE
Rich Flanagan rode for 4 hours 10 minutes around the track at Lindale Middle School in Linthicum, Maryland, on just the back wheel of his bicycle. He covered 50.5 mi (80.8 km) and only stopped when a sudden gust of wind knocked him off balance.

BAG RAFT
In 2014, a group of South Korean students protested against the amount of air found in potato chip packets by building a raft out of 160 unopened bags and paddling it for 0.8 mi (1.3 km) across the Han River.

FLAMING HOOPS
Casey Martin, one half of the KamiKaze FireFlies performance duo, spun five flaming hula hoops, with a total of 20 blazing torch heads, around her body simultaneously at the Ohio Renaissance Festival near Waynesville on September 29, 2019.

STRETCH NOODLE
Japanese chef Hiroshi Kuroda prepared a single egg noodle that was 602.75 ft (184 m) long—just over twice the length of a football field. He soaked the noodle in sesame oil before cooking to prevent it from breaking.

COOL COLLECTION
Lori-Ann Keenan, of Vancouver, British Columbia, Canada, has collected more than 2,000 pairs of sunglasses.

POLE POSITION
Vernon Kruger spent 78 days 23 hours 14 minutes living in a 132-gal (600-l) wine barrel perched atop an 82-ft-tall (25-m) pole in Dullstroom, South Africa. He survived on food and water hoisted up to him by a pulley system but had a narrow escape when a bolt of lightning struck the side of his barrel. When he finally decided to come down in February 2020, he was airlifted from his perch by helicopter. Back in 1997, Kruger spent 67 days sitting atop a pole.

By the end of WWII, the Federal Bureau of Investigation, or FBI, had a physical database of over 10 million fingerprints— the filing cabinets filled an area larger than a football field!

No two people in the world have the same fingerprints—not even identical twins, who are genetically indistinguishable. Fingerprints don't change with age and will even grow back from minor injuries! That's why they have been used as a nearly foolproof way of identifying people, particularly criminals, for hundreds of years. It used to take a trained eye to study the loops, whorls, and arches of a print to confirm a match. Today, fingerprints can be scanned and compared digitally and are used in the most everyday of tasks, like unlocking a phone.

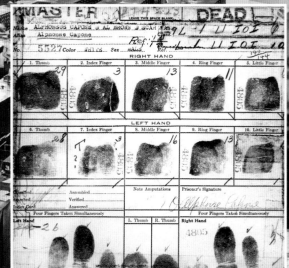

Fingerprint card of notorious gangster Al Capone, a.k.a. Scarface.

A fingerprint examiner at work.

VINYL FLOORING

Vinyl is a popular flooring choice for many homeowners, but vinyl records are usually reserved for the turntable. Not so for Sonia Barton of Derbyshire, England, who couldn't find any tile to match her vibrant personality, so she made her own by upcycling dozens of records, thousands of flower-shaped buttons, and a few handfuls of coins!

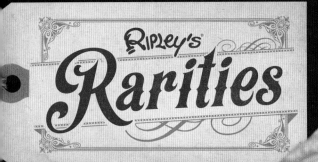

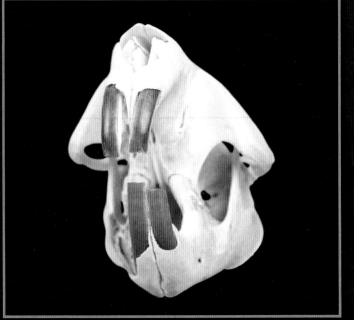

Ripley's Exhibit
Cat. No. 174585

BEAVER SKULL

The beaver is the largest rodent in North America, with teeth that never stop growing and are worn down by chewing down trees for their dams.

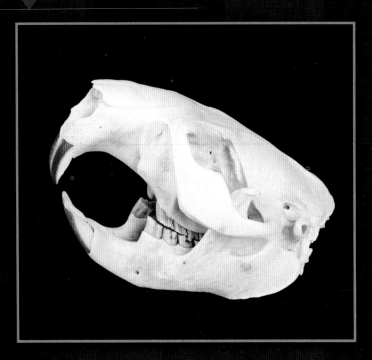

Ripley's Exhibit
Cat. No. 16065

BAT TOOTH NECKLACE

Made with dozens of teeth from flying foxes—
one of the largest types of bats on Earth.

Ripley's Exhibit
Cat. No. 174293

SPLIT-JAW GAR

Alligator gar born with a
split lower jaw complete
with four rows of teeth.
The fish gets its name
from its long mouth, sharp
teeth, and hard scales.

FAN FEED

ORDER UP

Noah Sheidlower of Great Neck, New York, shared with us his impressive collection of more than 6,000 takeout menus! He started collecting them when he was 12, when he saved a menu from an empanada restaurant—which he still has—and is now attending Columbia University. Over the years, he has managed to collect menus from about 20 U.S. states and countries as far as Israel. Sheidlower tells us that he is in the process of sorting the menus into a spreadsheet and estimates there are at least 70–80 different cuisines represented in his collection, including Korean-Uzbek fusion!

Alice Pang from Hong Kong only started work as a fashion model at age 93 and has since done photo shoots for high-end brands such as Gucci and Valentino.

THIMBLE COLLECTION

Gladys Minter, from Hampshire, England, has collected nearly 27,000 finger thimbles since 1980. She has thimbles made of wood, rubber, leather, pewter, and yarn, including one topped with a miniature greenhouse.

KNEE STRIKES

Five-year-old Aashman Taneja, from Hyderabad, India, made more than 1,200 one-leg, full contact tae kwon do knee strikes in one hour.

SENIOR MEDIC

In 2019, Christian Chenay was still working as a doctor and treating patients in Chevilly-Larue, France, at age 98. He started his career as a doctor back in 1951.

EPIC SWIM

In September 2019, cancer survivor Sarah Thomas, from Conifer, Colorado, became the first person to swim the English Channel four times non-stop, covering 130 mi (208 km) in 54 hours. Her planned distance was around 80 mi (128 km), but strong currents between England and France kept pulling her off course.

MAYO LOVER

Even though she is a petite 112 lb (50 kg), competitive eater Michelle Lesco, from Tucson, Arizona, can eat three and a half jars of mayonnaise in only three minutes.

HORROR HEARSE

Artist Karl Claydon, from Murwillumbah, Australia, spent 10 months transforming an old 1983 Ford Falcon hearse into a mobile house of horrors, complete with gothic windows and eerie midnight cemetery scenes that feature a coffin protruding from the soil and spiders climbing over cracked headstones. He uses the Transylvanian castle on wheels not only to transport his artworks but also to drive his mother to church or to the doctor's office.

BASEBALL CARDS

Paul Jones, of Idaho Falls, Idaho, began collecting baseball cards over 25 years ago and has now amassed more than 2.7 million.

HEAD ACROBAT

Chinese acrobat Li Longlong climbed 36 stairs while balancing on his head. He made his ascent by bouncing his head up from one step to the next, taking care to ensure he did not touch the steps with anything other than his head.

BACON FEAST

In only 25 minutes, British food blogger Kate Ovens ate "The Baconator," a hot dog layered in cheese and bacon that at 3 ft (0.9 m) long was more than half her height.

OPEN-CAKE SURGERY

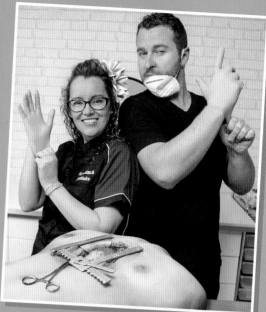

Nina and John Blackburn from Auckland, New Zealand, have crafted a "heart-stopping" cardiac surgery cake for their local hospital.

The Blackburns' gory confection features chocolate cake stuffed with hazelnut truffle filling. Covered in hazelnut ganache, the open-heart masterpiece showcases edible, flesh-colored airbrushing. Diluted strawberry jam and red food coloring add a touch of horror. Whimsical cake toppers include a rib spreader, red-filled tubes, and surgical tools and clamps. Even the chocolate "surgical instruments" are dusted with metallic food-grade paint.

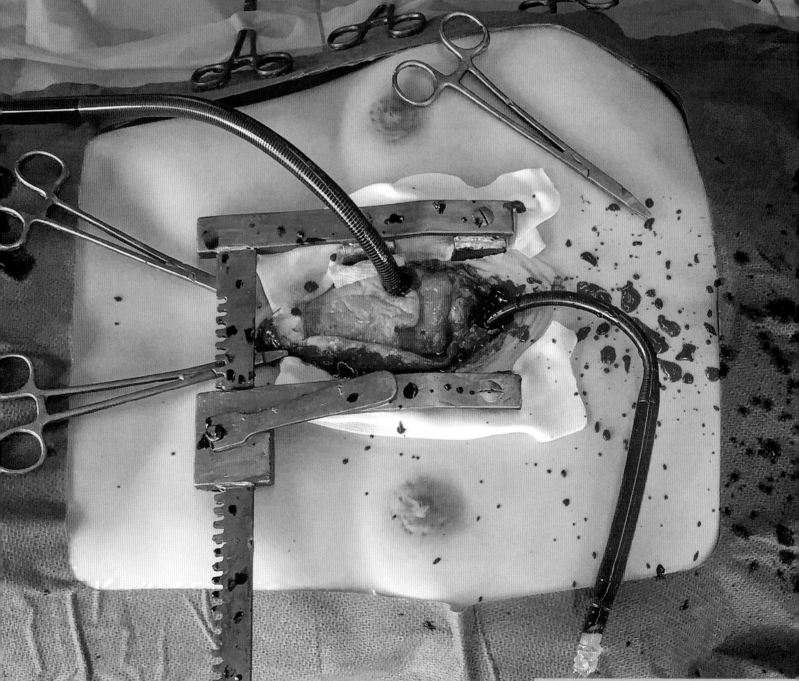

WAVE RAVE

You're not looking at aliens from a science-fiction movie; these are actual creatures living in our oceans!

Underwater photographer and marine biologist Simon Pierce of New Plymouth, New Zealand, captured these colors—normally invisible to the human eye—by using a special light and filter. The neon hues are a result of biofluorescence. Unlike bioluminescence, in which creatures like fireflies produce their own light, biofluorescence is when an organism absorbs light and re-emits it at a different wavelength. With a yellow filter, Pierce was able to remove the blue light that typically overpowers the human eye and reveal this unique characteristic.

Pierce's complicated camera setup used to capture these images.

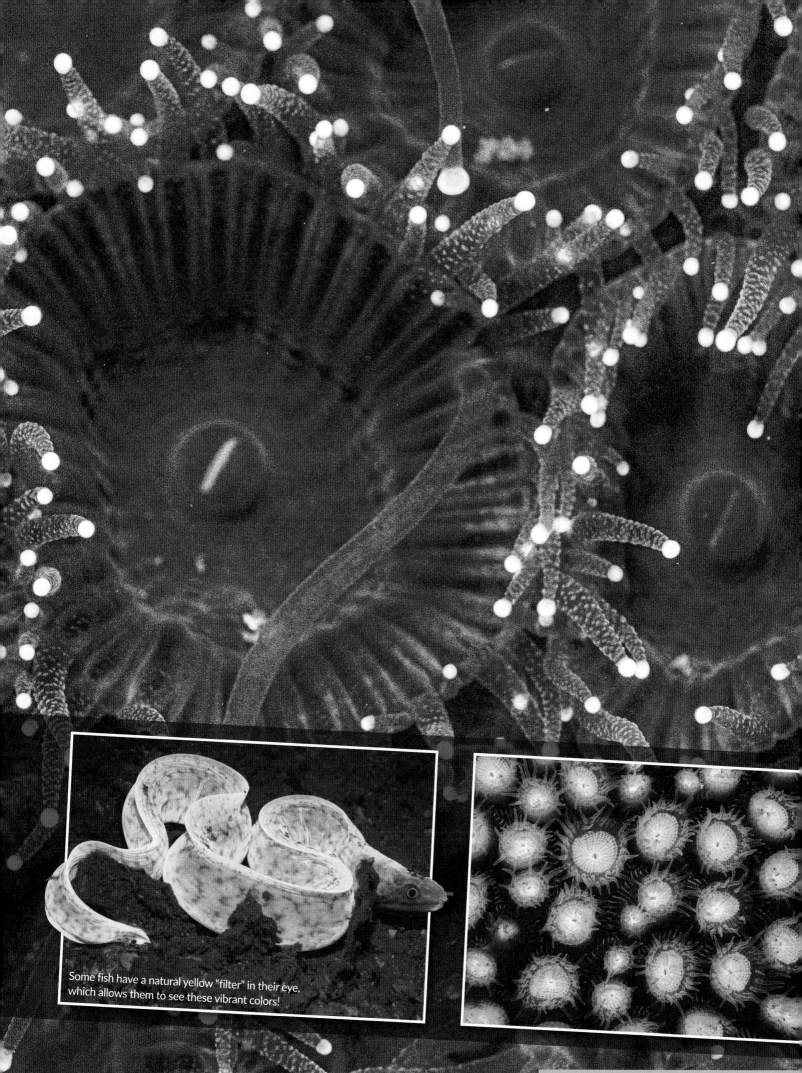

Some fish have a natural yellow "filter" in their eye, which allows them to see these vibrant colors!

PINK DRINK

Cafés and street vendors in the Himalayan region of Kashmir sell pink tea called Kashmiri chai. Starting out as green tea, the addition of baking soda turns it deep maroon. The liquid is then shocked with ice to preserve the color, and finally, when milk is added, it becomes bright pink. Although it looks like a strawberry milkshake, it has a salty, savory taste.

MISSING WORDS

There is not a word for either "yes" or "no" in Ireland's Gaelic language.

GOURD HATS

The Ilocano people of Northern Luzon, in the Philippines, wear hats made out of gourds. The headgear—known as a *tabungaw* hat—is often worn by farmers to protect them from the sun while they are working in the fields.

MOLD MARVEL

The slime mold *Physarum polycephalum* has no brain but almost 720 sexes. It has no mouth, no stomach, no legs, and no eyes, but it can detect food and digest it. If cut in half, the *Physarum polycephalum* heals itself within two minutes!

DEAD END

Although it is only 16 mi (25 km) long and, for the most part, less than 1 mi (1.6 km) wide, the island of Ocracoke, located in the Outer Banks off the coast of North Carolina, is home to more than 80 cemeteries.

INSECT MENU

The Insect Experience, a restaurant in Cape Town, South Africa, serves only food made from bugs. The menu includes mopane worm polenta fries, black fly larvae chickpea croquettes, and dried mealworms. It was conceived by Gourmet Grubb, a company that also produces a dairy-free ice cream made from black soldier fly larvae.

PIZZA ORIGIN

The Hawaiian pizza did not originate in Hawaii but in Canada. It was invented in 1962 by Sam Panopoulos for his restaurant, The Satellite, in Chatham, Ontario.

74 LETTERS

The Khmer alphabet in Cambodia has 74 letters, including 33 consonants, 23 vowels, and 12 independent vowels. Words in a sentence are written in a long, continuous line without any spaces between them.

CAVE COURT

Residents of Xinchun village in rural China play basketball inside of a massive cave! The decision to build a court inside the karst cavern was born out of a desire to preserve land for growing crops. Thanks to the cave's natural insulation, it remains a comfortable temperature all year long!

WOAH, CHRISTMAS TREE!

In an effort to create a new holiday tradition, Dutch artist Leon de Bruijne and designer Willem van Doorn built a cannon that shoots Christmas trees!

The *Kerstboomkanon*, or Christmas Tree Cannon, uses air pressure to fire the festive firs through the air in a flurry of green needles, much to the delight of onlookers. The furthest distance a tree has flown is 210 ft (64 m)! Since the cannon has been used every holiday season since 2016, it's well on its way to becoming a yearly tradition.

CHILD BAN

Doctors in Uganda have banned Mariam Nabatanzi from having any more children. She had already given birth to 44 by the time she was 36, including five sets of quadruplets, five sets of triplets, and four pairs of twins.

LIVE LEECHES

A man in Longyan, China, who complained of non-stop coughing for two months, was found to have a live leech attached to his throat and another one living in his right nostril. He had probably swallowed them while drinking water from a mountain stream.

DEVIL HORN

Shyam Lal Yadav had a hard, 4-in-long (10-cm) "devil horn" removed from the top of his head by surgeons in Sagar, India. The sebaceous horn was made of keratin, the substance found in toenails and human hair, and had been growing for five years after he bumped his head.

HAIRY GUMS

A woman in Italy has hair growing out of her gums. The eyelash-like hairs were growing from both her upper and lower gums before doctors removed them from her mouth in 2009, but they then returned six years later. The rare condition—only the fifth case to be reported—is believed to be the result of a hormonal disorder.

In the 1920s, U.S. anti-prohibitionists simulated the taste of bourbon by adding dead rats to moonshine and letting them ferment for a few days.

OLYMPIC GOLD

The first American woman to win an Olympic gold medal was Margaret Abbott, who finished first in the women's golf tournament in Paris in 1900. But she had no idea at the time that she was competing in the Olympics and lived her whole life (she died in 1955) without ever finding out.

MIRACLE TWINS

Liliya Konovalova, from Uralsk, Kazakhstan, had twin babies an incredible 11 weeks apart—a one-in-50-million occurrence. She has a rare double uterus and gave birth to a premature girl, Liya, on May 24, 2019, and then to Liya's twin brother, Maxim, more than two months later on August 9.

BOTTLE VOYAGE

On May 14, 1983, 11-year-old Jenny Brown, from Jonesport, Maine, threw a bottle containing a message into the ocean—and 36 years later, it was found buried in the sand by a man walking along Cape Cod beach in Massachusetts.

TINY TOWNS

A staple of many seaside towns in the early 1960s, British model villages attracted more than 60 million visitors worldwide. Tourists are granted a bird's-eye-view of both real and fictional towns, many of which are extremely detailed. Some of the first model villages date back to seventh-century Japan, when Empress Suiko commissioned a garden crafted with an artificial depiction of Mount Sumeru. Today, the tradition lives on in iconic models like Bekonscot in Beaconsfield, Buckinghamshire, which is the oldest continually open model village.

POTENT RODENT

During World War II, Allied spies created exploding "rat bombs" in an attempt to destroy German factories.

A stranger-than-fiction footnote in history, British scientists in the 1940s stuffed dozens of dead rats with fuses, detonators, and explosives. They tasked the French Resistance with scattering these bomb-wielding vermin in German manufacturing plants. Their hope was that factory workers would dispose of the rat carcasses in their furnaces, triggering massive explosions. But before the plan could wreak havoc on Nazi-occupied France, the Germans discovered the plot before it could be implemented. Nevertheless, it caused a wild-goose chase on the part of the Germans to "exterminate" the bomb infestation.

SEAL WITH IT

Artist Claire Eason of Nottinghamshire, UK, used a garden rake to create a 300-foot-long image of a seal on Beadnell Bay in Northumberland. Eason started with a sketch, transforming it into an image so large it can only be seen from above.

SNOW CRAB

A snow crab with a 5.7-in (14.6-cm) shell that was caught in Japan in 2019 sold at auction to a Tokyo restaurant for $46,000.

LAST SPEAKER

Upon the death of her sister Wilma in 2017, Jessie Ross became the last speaker in the world of East Sutherland Gaelic, the native language of three fishing villages in northeast Scotland—Brora, Golspie, and Embo. When American linguist Nancy Dorian began studying the dialect in 1963, there were still more than 200 speakers.

SNOW BAN

After 162 in (4.1 m) of snow fell on Syracuse, New York, during the winter of 1991, the city's common council unanimously approved a resolution expressly banning any further snowfall until December 24, 1992.

STATE PRIDE

Pluto is still officially recognized as a planet in Illinois. Three years after it was controversially downgraded to a dwarf planet, the state decreed that Pluto should be restored to its former status to mark its discovery in 1930 by Clyde Tombaugh, who was born on a farm near Streator, Illinois.

GIGANTIC BAR

Ahead of Super Bowl LIV in 2020, Mars Wrigley unveiled a giant 2-ft-tall (0.6-m), 2.1-ft-wide (0.7-m) Snickers bar at its plant in Waco, Texas. It contained more than 1,200 lb (545 kg) of caramel, peanuts, and nougat, plus 3,500 lb (1,589 kg) of chocolate, and was the size of 43,000 regular Snickers bars.

MUSTARD DESSERT

In 2019, to commemorate National Mustard Day in the United States, food companies French's and Coolhaus teamed up to introduce mustard-flavored ice cream.

OFFICIAL LANGUAGE

Even though it has been used in government and education for more than a century, Swedish did not become the official language of Sweden until 2009.

DIVINE INTERVENTION

The 108-ft-tall (33-m) statue *Christ the King* in Świebodzin, Poland, had internet antennas installed on its golden crown in 2018 for unverified reasons—possibly to create a network for a video surveillance system. However, the bishop later ordered the removal of the antennas because many parishioners found them offensive.

NAZCA LINES

Located in the arid Peruvian coastal plains, the Nazca Lines were etched into the ground between 500 BC and 500 AD, and they remain among the most extraordinary archaeological enigmas of all time.

Known as geoglyphs, they depict more than 800 straight lines, 300 geometric figures, and 70 stylized animal and plant designs. Some lines stretch upward of 30 mi (48 km), and the plant and animal motifs range in length from 50 to 1,200 ft (15 to 366 m). The first Peruvian archaeologist to systematically study Nazca lines was Toribio Mejia Xesspe in 1926. Unable to identify them from the ground, planes soon crisscrossed the skies for an aerial perspective.

Xesspe was followed by American professor Paul Kosok, who declared that certain portions of the lines were effectively "the largest astronomy book in the world" in 1941. But the researcher who would have the most profound impact on our understanding of these designs remains German-born Peruvian mathematician Maria Reiche. Reiche earned the moniker "the Lady of the Lines" for her 40 years of dedicated study. In the process, she developed theories about the lines' calendrical and astronomical purposes.

Despite almost 100 years of modern research into these geoglyphs and their designation as a UNESCO World Heritage Site in 1994, researchers still have more questions than answers regarding these elaborate creations.

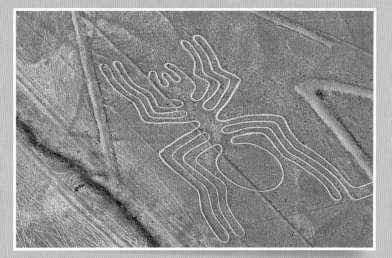

Believe it or not, this roughly 2,000-year-old, 121-ft-long (27-m) cat-shaped design was only discovered in October 2020!

FEROCIOUS FUNGI

These insects aren't wearing silly hats or fancy costumes—they have all been overtaken by fungus!

There are about 144,000 classified species of fungus, including different types of mushrooms, molds, yeasts, and others. Some of the most brutal varieties are called *entomopathogenic fungi*; these are parasites that take over an insect's body, sometimes even controlling its movements! The fungus grows within and around the host's body, resulting in bizarre growths and usually the insect's death. When it is done growing, the fungus releases spores, ready to infect its next victim.

EVEN TARANTULAS
CAN BE CONSUMED
BY FUNGI!

DEEP-SEA TERROR!

SOMETHING'S FISHY

Some of the weirdest creatures in the world can be found underwater.

1 Short Life
The female Pacific blackdragon fish grows to eight times the size of her male counterpart. The male dies soon after mating.

2 Colorless Blood
Due to a lack of red blood cells and hemoglobin, the crocodile icefish of the southern oceans has colorless blood.

3 Hanging Stomach
The deep-sea black swallower fish is able to eat prey more than twice its size in one bite by digesting it slowly in a large, expandable stomach that hangs below its body.

4 Electric Shock
Found off the Atlantic coast of North America, the northern stargazer fish burrows its body into sand before electrocuting passing fish or crustaceans and then swallowing them whole. It has a special organ behind its eyes that can transmit an electric shock powerful enough to stun small prey.

5 Big Mouth
The sarcastic fringehead fish, which lives off the Pacific coast of North America, has a mouth that can open to more than twice the width of its body. When rival males get too close, they unfurl their gigantic, brightly colored mouths and gape aggressively at each other. The one with the biggest mouth wins the standoff.

6 Jumping Fish
Piraputanga fish in South American rivers are able to leap several feet out of the water to snatch and eat berries from overhanging trees.

7 Tripod Fish
The deep-sea tripod fish gets its name from the three long, bony fins on which it rests at the bottom of the ocean while hunting for food. These fins can be 3.3 ft (1 m) long—three times the length of the fish's body.

8 Fish Armor
The hard scales of the *Arapaima gigas* fish that lives in the Amazon basin act as armor to withstand deadly piranha bites. This defense mechanism is so effective that scientists have used the design of the fish's scales to develop new types of body armor to protect humans against bullets and knife attacks.

FEELING TIRED

A crocodile in Palu, Indonesia, has been swimming around with a motorcycle tire around its neck for more than four years.

Fearful that the rubber ring will injure or strangle the reptile, wildlife officials have been trying to remove the tire for years. Believe it or not, a cash prize has been offered to anyone brave enough to remove the rubber ring from the 13-ft-long (4-m) croc.

To raise awareness, a local bakery made loaves of bread in the shape of the crocodile.

Ripley's Rarities

**Ripley's Exhibit
Cat. No. 175120**

ABRAHAM LINCOLN'S HAIR

A thick, two-inch tuft of hair clipped from President Abraham Lincoln's head the day after he was assassinated. Also part of this exhibit is the blood-stained telegram that was used to hold the hair.

IS THIS THE GUN THAT SHOT LINCOLN?

**Ripley's Exhibit
Cat. No. 17526**

JOHN WILKES BOOTH'S GUN

One of two pocket pistols, or derringers, carried by John Wilkes Booth on the night he assassinated President Lincoln. For years, it was unknown which one was used to kill Lincoln. Thanks to modern forensics, we now know the murder weapon is the one on display at Ford's Theatre in Washington, D.C.

PENNY PORTRAIT

Likeness of Abraham Lincoln created with 2,400 pennies. The differences in color on the coins were caused by exposure and usage. Created by Danny Haber of New Rochelle, New York.

SCARED STIFF

Bizarre and surreal sculptures are peppered throughout "Parco dei Mostri," a sixteenth-century horror show situated within an idyllic garden in Bomarzo, Italy. Known as "Garden of the Monsters" in English, the park was commissioned in 1552 by Prince Pier Francesco Orsini, as a visual representation of the harrowing experiences he faced, from warfare to captivity and death. The architect, Pirro Ligorio, realized the Prince's vision with statues like a three-headed dog, a dragon fighting a wolf and lion, and a war elephant. Perhaps the most chilling is a massive, screaming head with an inscription that reads "All reason departs."

FLYING DOCTORS

Australia's Royal Flying Doctor Service has 71 airplanes that soar more than 17 million mi (27 million km) every year to treat patients in remote locations—equivalent to 34 trips to the moon and back.

DYING LANGUAGE

The Njerep language is spoken only in Nigeria and by just four people, the youngest of whom is about 60 years old.

ANCIENT PASTRIES

The British Museum has an exhibit of preserved Chinese pastries that are more than 1,300 years old.

TWO SUNSETS

The 2,717-ft-high (828-m) Burj Khalifa tower in Dubai, United Arab Emirates, is so tall that visitors can watch the sunset twice. They can observe the sunset from the ground, and then by taking the elevator to the top of the building, they can watch it again, three minutes later.

ALPINE STADIUM

The Ottmar Hitzfeld Stadium, the home of Swiss soccer team FC Gspon, is perched on a mountainside 6,560 ft (2,000 m) above sea level. Players and fans must take two cable cars to reach the stadium, and the drop from the pitch is so steep that the club has lost more than 1,000 balls.

HOT MAIL

Visitors to the Pacific island of Vanuatu can send a postcard from an active volcano. The 1,184-ft-high (361-m) Mount Yasur volcano on the island of Tanna has erupted almost continuously for 800 years, but there is a mailbox near the crater's fiery rim and a mail carrier checks it frequently.

LIBRARY COLLECTION

There are more than 170 million items in the British Library. They occupy 466 mi (746 km) of shelving—the equivalent of the distance from London to Aberdeen, Scotland—and the basement goes as far underground as the height of an eight-story building. A visitor viewing five items per day would take more than 80,000 years to see the whole collection.

GOING UP?

The Bailong Elevator, located on a cliffside in China's Zhangjiajie National Forest Park, is more than 1,000 ft (205 m) tall!

Known alternately as the Hundred Dragons Elevator, it boasts three double-decker elevators that climb the side of a sandstone pillar. Just under half of its height is located within the mountain itself, with the remaining top-half exposed to stunning yet hair-raising views. Each elevator carries up to 50 people and takes about two minutes to reach the top. In 2013, French climber Jean-Michel Casanova scaled the outer section of the steel structure—564 ft (172 m)— in 68 minutes 26 seconds with no safety equipment.

OLM, MY!

Olms are blind, cave-dwelling salamanders that can live to at least 100 years old! The first written record of the olm is from 1689, when heavy rains caused the amphibians to be flushed out of their caves. Their long bodies and stubby arms inspired the belief that they may have been baby dragons. But these are not fierce creatures. Olms only grow up to 12 in (30.5 cm) long and are slow-moving. Most only move around 16 ft (4.9 m) per year, but a recent study found that one individual did not move for seven entire years!

SNOT PALACES

Small 4-in-long (10-cm), ocean-dwelling, tadpole-like creatures called giant larvaceans build complex homes around themselves by secreting mucus from cells on their heads. These "snot palaces" can be up to 3.3 ft (1 m) wide, the equivalent of a human building a five-story house. The near-transparent houses protect the creature from predators but are so delicate they quickly become clogged and a new one usually has to be constructed every day.

ZOMBIE ANTS

The deadly *Ophiocordyceps unilateralis* fungus feeds on ants from the inside, eventually completely taking over their bodies, turning their hosts into zombie ants and causing spores to burst out from them.

TAIL LIGHTS

Horseshoe crabs have a total of 10 eyes distributed around their body, including a series of light sensors along the top and side of their tail.

DOUBLE DAVE

A baby timber rattlesnake with two heads, two tongues, four eyes but only one body was found in a forest in New Jersey's Pine Barrens. Studies revealed that both of the snake's fully formed heads pulled in different directions at the same time due to its independently operating brains, but the right head was more dominant. The reptile was given the name "Double Dave" after David Schneider and Dave Burkett, the two herpetologists who discovered it.

Female Komodo dragons can sometimes give birth without mating with a male—a process called *parthenogenesis*. But only male baby dragons can be born in this way.

TOP DOG

Bucca, a rescue dog found on the streets in upstate New York, is now a key member of the New York City Fire Department with special responsibility for detecting any accelerants that may indicate arson. Bucca was given a special bravery award in 2019 and was also named the top dog in the whole of the United States for detecting accelerants.

LOUD CALL

The male white bellbird of South America produces a mating call that measures 125 decibels—louder than a chainsaw or a jackhammer.

DESERT RACERS

The Saharan silver ant can run 108 times the length of its own body every second—similar to a human running 400 mph (644 kmph).

CONFUSED SNAKE

Kronos, an eastern kingsnake at the Forgotten Friend Reptile Sanctuary in Elm, Pennsylvania, had to be rescued from itself when it tried to swallow 10 in (25 cm) of its own tail. Confused kingsnakes sometimes bite their own tail in the belief that it's another snake, but they typically let go once they realize their mistake and hardly ever attempt to actually swallow it.

TEGU TALENT

THE ARTIST!

Winston the Argentine black and white tegu creates artworks by dipping his claws and tail in colored paint and thrashing against a white canvas.

The affectionate lizard is owned by Sarah Curry of Lansing, Michigan, who adopted Winston after he was abandoned in a box at The Great Lakes Zoological Society. Argentine black and white tegus can grow to more than 4 ft (1.2 m) long and are known to be relatively docile pets. Exotic pets like tegus often require more care than owners anticipate and sometimes end up in poor health, released into the wild, or dumped at an animal facility, like Winston was. Winston's paintings sell for up to $75 each and have raised thousands of dollars toward the Australian Bushfire Fund.

COPIOUS CANINES

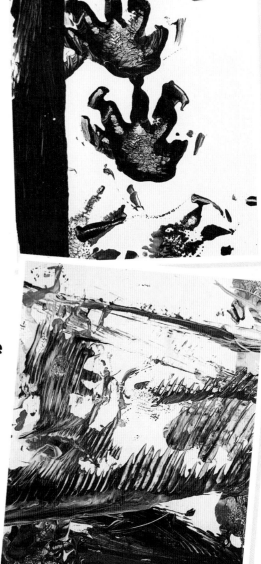

Loki the Great Dane of Tulsa, Oklahoma, had 70 teeth in his mouth—28 more than normal! Loki was about one year old when he was taken to the veterinarian for a routine checkup, which is when his dental anomaly was discovered. His owner suspected he had extra teeth, but had never been able to take a long look in the rambunctious puppy's mouth; however, they never thought he had literally dozens too many! The vet was able to remove 21 of the extra chompers, leaving Loki with a much more comfortable smile.

DENIM DREAMS

London-based artist Ian Berry creates large installations, portraits, and urban scenery using little more than denim from recycled jeans.

Berry's images are so realistic that many people mistake them for blue-toned photographs at first glance. A closer inspection reveals the many layers and shades of denim used to craft each masterpiece. He has more than 2,000 pairs of jeans, from which he chooses the exact shade of blue required. His latest artistic series, *Hotel California*, explores the "Golden State" in pop culture. Through each collage's blue filter, Berry examines the dichotomy between proverbial California and its lived reality.

SHACKLED SWIM

With his hands and feet shackled, 70-year-old Jack LaLanne swam while towing 70 people in 70 rowboats from Queensway Bridge in Long Beach, California, to the ship *Queen Mary* in 1984. He covered the distance of 1 mi (1.6 km) in two and a half hours, battling all the way against strong winds and currents. Known as the "Godfather of Fitness," LaLanne achieved many remarkable physical feats throughout his life, such as doing 1,000 push-ups and 1,000 chin-ups in just 86 minutes! He ate his last dessert in 1929 and passed away in 2011, at 96 years old.

BALCONY MARATHON

During the COVID-19 lockdown, French athlete Elisha Nochomovitz ran an entire 26.2-mi (42-km) marathon on the 23-ft-long (7-m) balcony outside his apartment in Balma. It took him 6 hours 48 minutes to complete about 3,000 laps of his balcony.

LEGO SETS

Matt Hines, from Evans, Georgia, has a collection of nearly 1,200 LEGO Star Wars sets. He started collecting them more than 20 years ago in 1999.

PINEAPPLE SLICE

Syed Alavi, of Kerala, India, used a sword to slice through 75 pineapples being held on the heads of volunteers in less than 30 seconds.

SHARK PUNCH

While surfing at Pauanui Beach, New Zealand, 60-year-old Nick Minogue, from Auckland, fended off an attack by a great white shark by punching it in the eye. The shark left bite marks on his board and two tooth holes in his wetsuit.

BEAVER FEVER

Lori Gongaware, from Chesterfield, Virginia, has collected more than 1,400 beaver figurines since 1996. She has beaver bottle openers, coffee cups, stampers, pencil sharpeners, and even a tattoo.

WHEELCHAIR CROSSING

Eight years after he was paralyzed from the neck down as a result of a cycling accident, Ian Mackay rode his wheelchair 350 mi (560 km) across Washington State in 11 days.

GRANDFATHER SCORES

Egyptian soccer player Ezzeldin Bahader played a full 90-minute game and scored on his professional debut—at age 75. On March 7, 2020, the grandfather of six scored from the penalty spot to earn the Cairo-based October 6 club a 1-1 draw against Genius in the third tier of Egyptian soccer.

SOLAR POWER

During a 2019 heat wave in Perth, Western Australia, Stu Pengelly cooked a 3.3-lb (1.5-kg) pork roast just by leaving it in a baking tin on the seat of his car for 10 hours.

BOARD GAMES

David Przybyla, a professor of marketing at Utah Valley University, has a collection of about 2,000 board games. His interest started in 2008 after a coworker introduced him to the tile-building game Carcassonne, but he estimates that he has only played about 2 percent of his collection.

SKY HIGH

Humans have longed to fly since the dawn of time, but one thing that is often overlooked when daydreaming about reaching new heights is the trip back down. Here are some strange but true ways people and animals have "stuck the landing."

NEW SPORT

Miles Daisher of Twin Falls, Idaho, invented "skyaking"—skydiving while sitting in a kayak and landing on water.

DANGEROUS JOB

Smokejumpers are specialized firefighters who parachute into wildfires!

LUCKY LANDING

On September 25, 1999, skydiver Joan Murray survived a 14,500-foot drop after landing on a mound of fire ants, whose stings kept her alive!

RAINING RODENTS

To reduce the numbers of invasive snakes on the island of Guam, 2,000 mice laced with a drug lethal to the reptiles were airdropped with tiny parachutes over the nation!

LOST LEG

Chris Marckres lost his prosthetic leg while skydiving, but was reunited with it after Vermont farmer Joseph Marszalkowski discovered it intact and unharmed in a soybean field.

DAREDEVIL DOG

BASE jumper Bruno Valente has taken his border collie Kazuza with him on more than 40 BASE jumps!

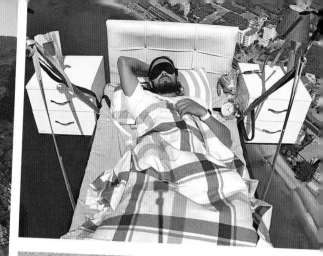

DOMESTIC FLIGHT

Hasan Kaval, a 29-year-old paragliding pilot and instructor from Izmir, Turkey, recently made couch surfing atmospheric with a sofa skydiving stunt.

To pull off the feat, Kaval customized a red leather sofa with a metal frame to which he attached wheels and a canopy. He also added a lamp, television, and footstool for good measure. Mid-flight, Kaval swapped out his shoes for slippers, sipped on a soda, and munched on some chips—all of this despite not being strapped into the makeshift flying couch machine.

Kaval's flying feats don't stop there. He has also performed such spectacular stunts as a paragliding while sleeping on a bed, playing a board game with a friend, and drinking coffee with an interviewer.

BOTTLE TREE
Villagers in Chekka, Lebanon, spent 20 days building a 28.5-ft-tall (8.7-m) Christmas tree using 129,000 plastic water bottles. It had taken them eight months to collect all the bottles needed for the tree.

NINE CANS
Shunichi Kanno of Japan is able to stick nine aluminum cans onto his face and head simultaneously just by using the air suction between the cans and his skin. He says the secret is to wrinkle the skin on the forehead, press the can firmly into place, then ease the wrinkle to reduce the air pressure between the can and skin, allowing for better suction.

WILDFIRE PHOTOGRAPHER
Noah Berger, a photographer based in San Francisco, California, has taken close-up pictures of more than 100 wildfires, getting within a couple of feet of 90-ft-high (27-m) flames. He once experienced a terrifying fire tornado that touched down only 0.75 mi (1.2 km) from him after it was driven on by unpredictable 140 mph (224 kmph) winds.

DAILY VISITOR
Jeff Reitz, of Huntington Beach, California, visited the state's Disneyland theme park every day for more than eight years. He went there for 2,995 days straight until the coronavirus pandemic forced the park to close temporarily in March 2020.

MARTIAL ARTIST
Pakistani martial artist Irfan Mehsood performed 70 jumping jacks in one minute while carrying an 80-lb (36-kg) pack. He has also completed 59 knuckle push-ups in one minute while carrying a 60-lb (27-kg) pack and did 40 push-ups in one minute with one leg raised while carrying an 80-lb (36-kg) pack.

URBAN JUNGLE
Joe Bagley keeps more than 1,400 potted houseplants in his one-bedroom apartment in Loughborough, England, including cacti, tropical flowers, ferns, and vines. He spends several hours each day feeding, watering, and tending to them.

成俊工業株式会社 ×武 株式会社 武田建設 Oni no Sumika. 鬼の栖 山建運輸株式会社

In Japan, the Nebuta festival showcases lantern-like floats constructed of painted *washi* paper and wireframes measuring up to 30 ft (9 m) wide by 16 ft (5 m) tall.

Locals devote a year to crafting the elaborate floats. Designs depict historical and mythical figures from Chinese and Japanese folklore. Some also portray *kabuki*—Japanese traditional theater—actors and even characters from popular TV shows. During the event, locals push each of the two dozen floats through the streets, weaving back and forth and spinning for the crowd. *Taiko* drummers, flutists, and hand-cymbal players accompany each float, along with hundreds of *haneto* dancers in traditional costume, making for an eye-popping spectacle.

STACKED UP

The social media user known as "Menga" achieved an unbelievable level of balance by stacking 1,002 Jenga blocks atop one vertical block! It took him less than 40 minutes to complete the topsy-turvy yet strangely beautiful tower. In the video Menga uploaded to YouTube as proof of his accomplishment, viewers can see that there was no glue or binding agents used, as he yanks the bottom piece out for a dramatic finish, allowing the structure to fall to pieces.

1,002 JENGA BLOCKS!

GENIE SPEAK
Robin Williams ad-libbed so much during recording sessions for the Genie in the 1992 movie *Aladdin* that the producers ended up with 16 hours of material.

DENTAL CARE
Charlotte Brontë spent some of her first earnings from her 1847 novel *Jane Eyre* on getting her teeth fixed.

CITY HONOR
Musician Usher has a road named after him—the Usher Raymond Parkway in Chattanooga, Tennessee, the city where he was raised.

TEA DRINKERS
In the course of the 12 novels and 20 short stories that feature English writer Agatha Christie's amateur detective Miss Marple, the characters drink 143 cups of tea.

PET PURCHASE
As a struggling actor, Sylvester Stallone was so poor that he sold his bull mastiff dog, Butkus, for $40 to a stranger outside a 7-Eleven store. When Stallone became rich by selling the script for *Rocky*, he waited outside the same store for three days for the new owner to show up and bought the dog back for $15,000.

TULIP DIET
Academy Award–winning actress Audrey Hepburn kept herself from starving during the German invasion of Holland in World War II by eating nettles and tulip bulbs.

ONLY NOVEL
English author Anna Sewell's 1877 book *Black Beauty* has sold more than 50 million copies, yet it was her only novel.

RAT BOOM
After the success of the 2007 animated film *Ratatouille*, sales of pet rats jumped by as much as 50 percent.

TONGUE-TIED

Two towering brontosauruses, one located on either side of a major highway near the town of Erenhot (a.k.a. Erlian) in China, appear to be stretching their long necks out to kiss each other.

Each dinosaur statue measures 112 ft (34 m) wide by 62 ft (19 m) tall. When measured from tail-to-tail, the combined work stretches 262 ft (80 m) across. The area, now part of the Gobi Desert, was once a paradise for dinosaurs, as evidenced by the myriad of fossils found in the region. On a visit to this Jurassic-sized landmark of love, you'll also notice many dozens of smaller dino statues of all shapes and sizes scattered on the ground.

CAT FRIENDLY
When English "nonsense" poet Edward Lear moved to San Remo, Italy, in the 1870s, he instructed the architect to build his new home as a replica of the old one to make the move easier for his beloved tailless cat Foss.

WALL DRAWING
Using black markers, Chinese artist Guo Feng created a 3,326-ft-long (1,014-m) black-and-white drawing on a canvas stretched out along the Simatai section of the Great Wall of China. It took him two months, working more than 10 hours a day and sometimes starting at 4 a.m.

GAMES LAUNCH
In 2019, video games *Pokémon Sword* and *Pokémon Shield* sold six million units worldwide during their launch weekend—sales of more than 1,380 games per minute.

SWEET INSPIRATION
The song "A Spoonful of Sugar" in *Mary Poppins* was inspired by a polio vaccine. Songwriter Robert Sherman's son, Jeffrey, came home one day and talked about the polio vaccine he had just received at school from a doctor who had made the medicine easier to take by dripping it onto a sugar cube.

YOUNG ARTIST
Twelve-year-old Xeo Chu from Vietnam does colorful, abstract paintings that sell for more than $150,000 USD—and in 2019, had his first solo exhibition in Manhattan. He started painting at age four and sold his first work when he was just six.

STAR STUDENT
H. G. Wells, who wrote the sci-fi novel *The War of the Worlds*, once worked as a math teacher at Henley House School in London, England, where one of his brightest students was A. A. Milne, the future author of *Winnie the Pooh*.

OUT OF PLACE

The grounds of Balmoral Castle contain a fascinating secret. The Scottish residence of Great Britain's royal family boasts a hidden pyramid! Built by none other than Queen Victoria, the Egyptian-inspired structure commemorates her husband and soulmate, Prince Albert, who died at 42 years old in 1861. To reach the memorial, visitors must take a woodland path around the estate's park, adding to the mystery of the clandestine monument.

TO THE BELOVED MEMORY OF ALBERT, THE GREAT AND GOOD PRINCE CONSORT. ERECTED BY HIS BROKEN HEARTED WIDOW VICTORIA R. 21ST AUGUST 1862

UNTIMELY TEAR

According to folklore, the small town of Black Ankle in San Augustine County, Texas, was named after a local woman who accidentally tore a hole in her black silk stocking at the ankle before a dance and tried to conceal the rip by painting it over with soot.

DANGEROUS JOB

Local fishermen earn their living by wading through crocodile-infested waters to catch fish just a few feet from the top of Africa's mighty Victoria Falls. One false step would send them plunging 350 ft (107 m) down the waterfall to certain death.

HIGH HAY

In Rishikesh, India, villagers build haystacks up in trees. Located in the foothills of the Himalayas, the region is one of the wettest places in North India, meaning the ground is always soggy during the monsoon months, so bundling the hay atop trees keeps it dry.

The "Dream Mine" near Salem, Utah, was first excavated by John Koyle in 1894 and has more than 7,000 stockholders—but has yet to produce so much as a tiny nugget of gold.

BREAD RESPECT

Bread is treated with such respect in Azerbaijan that if someone accidentally drops any on the floor, the custom is to pick it up and kiss it by way of an apology. Even when bread goes stale, Azerbaijanis don't simply throw it out. Instead, they separate it from the rest of the trash and hang it in bags to signify their respect.

VOLCANIC CHEESE

Saint-Nectaire cheese from the Auvergne region of France gets its unique flavor not only because it is made from the milk of cows that feed on rich, volcanic pastures, but also because it is stored in cellars carved from hardened volcanic ash. Seven thousand years ago, the area was home to active volcanoes that covered the countryside with lava.

PIRANHA RAMEN

From September 20 to 23, 2019, customers snapped up bowls of the world's first piranha ramen at Ninja Café & Bar in Tokyo, Japan. Customers could opt for a bowl of noodles with piranha broth but without the fish itself, or they could have the dish topped with a whole deep-fried piranha—teeth and all.

COOKIE CITY

Each year, residents of Bergen, Norway, craft a winter wonderland using more than 1,000 lb (454 kg) of *pepperkaker* (literally "pepper cracker"), or gingerbread.

The tradition began in 1991, and today thousands of volunteers participate in building the delicious cookie metropolis known as Pepperkakebyen. Over the decades, the display has expanded, both in terms of size and complexity. Take, for example, the 2019 construction, which consisted of 2,000 gingerbread buildings. Structures included a soccer stadium, trains, boats, and cars, weighing in at a whopping 1,320 lb (600 kg).

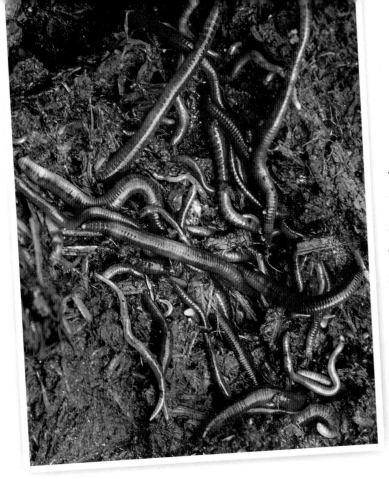

WEIRD WEATHER

You might have heard the phrase "it's raining cats and dogs" to describe a heavy downpour, but these weather phenomena are simply too strange for words!

1 Squirmy Mystery

Thousands of earthworms rained down on the snow-laden mountains of Southern Norway in 2015, baffling local biologists and meteorologists.

2 Chocolate Rain

After a ventilation defect at a Sprüngli and Lindt factory in Olten, Switzerland, cocoa powder dusted area residents.

3 Falling Fish

In Mexico, locals use phrases like *lluvia de peces* ("fish rain") and *aguacero de pescado* ("downpour of fish") to describe fish-laden precipitation, a phenomenon attributed to waterspouts.

4 Red Waters

In 2014–2015, residents of villages in northwest Spain noticed that the water in public fountains turned blood red following a rainstorm of microscopic, red pigment-producing algae.

5 Just Add Coffee

Non-dairy creamer poured from the heavens over Chester, South Carolina, in 1969, the aftermath of an exhaust system malfunction at a local factory.

6 Heavenly Riches

Precious metals and jewels fell from Siberia's skies in 2018 after an old transport plane carrying an estimated $368 million in platinum, diamonds, and gold spilled its contents during takeoff.

7 Fore!

Golf balls pelted confused Floridians in 1969 during an event that meteorologists later attributed to a tornado at a nearby golf course.

8 Spider Sprinkle

In an event known as ballooning, millions of tiny spiders rained from Australian skies in 2015, having released gossamer threads to catch the wind and disperse after hatching.

ICE VOLCANOES

During the frigid winter months near the shores of Lake Michigan, specific conditions can result in the formation of an unexpected sight—erupting ice volcanoes!

Unlike their searing, lava-filled counterparts, geology and plate tectonics don't fuel ice volcanoes. Instead, extreme cold weather combined with abundant water is the secret recipe. As temperatures drop in the dead of winter and the lake's surface freezes, waves beneath the ice sheet continue to push upward, creating cone-like projections on the surface. Over time, these waves erode openings at the peak of each cone, permitting icy water to spew spectacularly from the top.

WATERLESS BRIDGE

As Poyang Lake waters in China recede, a hidden treasure emerges—a 9,612-ft-long (2,930-m) Ming-era bridge named Qianyan. Crafted from granite, the bridge dates back nearly 400 years and reveals itself during the dry season, when water levels are low. Unfortunately, a combination of low rainfall and impacts from the Three Gorges Dam has depleted the lake, causing water levels to drop abnormally and threaten the local wildlife.

MOTION PICTURE PARK

Leicester Square in London, England, is peppered with bronze statues of famous movie characters!

The long-term art installment, titled "Scenes in the Square," celebrates a century of cinema, with each statue representing a different decade in film. From old-school comedy duo Laurel and Hardy's 1929 movie *Liberty*, all the way to 2020 with *Wonder Woman 1984*, visitors can learn about iconic characters such as Mary Poppins, Harry Potter, and even Paddington Bear through the accompanying audio tour. The Square itself, which often hosts extravagant red-carpet movie premieres, celebrated its 350th anniversary in 2020.

KNOCK KNOCK

Throughout the U.S. Capitol Building, there are tiny doors, about 30 in (76 cm) in height, that open up to reveal water faucets! In 1851, a fire tore through the building, burning up 35,000 books in the Library of Congress, including some from Thomas Jefferson's personal collection. An investigation revealed that if there had been a water source nearby, the fire could have been quickly extinguished. So, to prevent future disasters, a system of pipes was installed to bring water from the Potomac River into the Capitol. These hidden faucets also helped custodians keep the floors clean!

ANCIENT BEEF

The Metropolitan Museum of Art in New York City displays a preserved shoulder of beef, found in Luxor, Egypt, that is nearly 3,500 years old.

VALUABLE RAIN

In Botswana, the word for rain, "pula," is also the name of its national currency because, in a country where 70 percent of the territory is occupied by the Kalahari Desert, rain is very scarce and is therefore a valuable commodity.

COASTAL CITY

You can be standing on the coast of England in the center of London. This is because the North Sea ebbs and flows up and down the River Thames as far west as Teddington Lock, 78 mi (125 km) from the sea. Anywhere along the river up to that point, including Westminster and the London Eye, can reveal beaches at low tide.

RAT TRAP

The crypt of Christ Church Cathedral in Dublin, Ireland, contains a mummified cat chasing a mummified rodent. It is believed that the cat chased the rat into an organ pipe in the 1850s and both became trapped there.

LIGHT DESSERT

London-based design studio Bompas & Parr teamed up with German scientists to make an edible dessert that weighed just one gram. The meringue dessert was made of aerogel, one of the lightest solid materials in the world, and was 96 percent air.

MUSTACHE SAVER

Mustachioed men in the Victorian era used special teacups to protect their facial hair! Wax was often used to style their whiskers, but it could melt from the rising heat of a hot tea, causing perfectly groomed mustaches to droop. Enter the mustache cup: a mug with a little shelf that allowed tea to flow into the mouth but not the 'stache.

MAD MAX

Max, a black Labrador retriever, put his owner's car in reverse and drove it backward in circles for about an hour around a cul-de-sac in Port St. Lucie, Florida. The owner had gotten out of the car to ask for directions with the engine still running, but Max had then jumped into the front seat and hit the gear shift. This caused the transmission to shift into reverse, which also served to lock the car's doors. Max's joyride only ended when police officers arrived and were able to enter the unlock code into the driver's side keypad.

POOP PUMP

Silver-spotted skipper caterpillars use their blood pressure to pump their fecal pellets from an anal "launching pad" more than 4.5 ft (1.4 m) away from their nest to avoid attracting predators.

TODDLER RESCUE

Gatubela, a Siamese cat, saved one-year-old Samuel Léon from falling down a steep flight of stairs at his home in Bogotá, Colombia. Gatubela had been watching Samuel's movements closely, and when the toddler crawled toward the top of the stairs, the cat suddenly leapt from its seat, wrapped its paws around Samuel's body, and forced him away from danger.

HAPPY REUNION

Katheryn Strang's toy fox terrier Dutchess disappeared from her home in Orlando, Florida, in 2007 and was found 12 years later in Pittsburgh, Pennsylvania, more than 1,000 mi (1,600 km) away.

GOLDEN RAE

When Rae, a golden retriever, was born, a birth injury contributed to the loss of her left ear. As she grew, her right ear migrated to the top of her head, resulting in a unique, unicorn-like appearance. This, plus her happy-go-lucky attitude and ability to overcome obstacles, has garnered love and support from nearly 200,000 Instagram followers, and her TikTok videos have earned millions of views. Oh, and her name? It's "ear" backward.

OFF THE HOOK

Terri Olah, a diving guide in Jupiter, Florida, removes hooks from the mouths of sharks, no anesthetic required! Most people would agree the last place you want to stick your hand during an ocean dive is inside a shark's mouth. But Olah has no such misgivings. Upon spotting one of the massive marine predators with a fishing hook protruding from its jaw, she grabs it by the tail and turns it to immobilize it. Then, using a pair of pliers, she removes the hook while managing to keep all ten fingers

BAT BOOM

There are more than 1,200 species of bat, meaning that around 25 percent of all mammal species on Earth are bats.

PUPPY LOVE

When her micro-chipped Australian shepherd pup Jackson was taken from outside a grocery store in San Francisco, California, Emilie Talermo spared no expense in her attempt to get her dog back. She launched a GoFundMe account to offer a $7,000 reward, designed countless missing dog posters, and even spent $1,200 to fly an airplane banner over the city—and it all paid off, because four months later Jackson was safely returned.

ADVENTURE CHICKEN

Scrumper the adventure chicken from Fareham, England, joins her owner, Eryk Rose, on kayaking, tightrope-walking, and motorbiking activities. Even at home, she regularly perches on his shoulder and also happily sits on his robot vacuum cleaner while he guides it around the house.

BUCKET HEAD

A young eastern gray kangaroo in Queensland, Australia, spent at least five months with a bucket stuck on its head. The animal, which was nicknamed "Bucket Head," had the handle of a black plastic tub wrapped around its neck, probably after looking into it in search of food. Rescuers tried without success to capture the kangaroo, but despite the presence of the bucket, it was still able to eat and drink.

SHY PANDAS

For 10 years, the Ocean Park zoo in Hong Kong had been trying unsuccessfully to encourage its two resident giant pandas, Ying Ying and Le Le, to mate—but in April 2020, with the zoo in lockdown and no visitors around, the pair finally did.

TWO FACES

Duo the black kitten was born with one body, but has two faces, two noses, two mouths, and four eyes due to a rare craniofacial condition called *diprosopus*. Her middle two eyes fused into one large eye, which was surgically removed for her health. Adopted by San Diego, California, veterinarian Dr. Ralph Tran, Duo breathes through both noses and eats and meows with both mouths, sometimes separately and sometimes simultaneously. Some Janus cats, as they are known, meow from one mouth while at the same time eating with the other.

SNAKE COUPLING

On the day before Valentine's Day 2020, a section of a park in Lakeland, Florida, was closed to the public after large numbers of nonvenomous water snakes gathered there for mating.

COOL CAT

Jasper's hairless, eyeless appearance caused many to do a double-take, but he lived large despite the odds.

With more than 90,000 followers on Instagram, Jasper (a.k.a. Jazzy) lives on as an internet inspiration. He lived in Maine with his owner Kelli, who received him in 2009 as a Christmas gift. In 2013, Jasper lost an eye due to a flare-up of the feline herpes virus that progressed into a corneal ulcer. Five years later, Jazzy lost his second eye to the same disease. Despite these setbacks, he enjoyed an excellent quality of life, including the friendship of two rescue cat pals, until he passed in November 2020.

Ripley's Rarities

Ripley's Exhibit
Cat. No. 173335

GUNPOWDER ART

Created for Ripley's by Dino Tomic of Norway, this artwork was made by carefully arranging gunpowder across a wooden board. By lighting the powder, the image was burned into the wood, leaving a permanent picture.

Ripley's Exhibit
Cat. No. 173067

TORTOISE SHELL SHIELD

This shield is crafted from the shell of a giant land tortoise. Antelope antlers serve as the handles, and can also be used like a bayonet.

Ripley's Exhibit
Cat. No. 174583

"GREEK FIRE" HAND GRENADE

Eighth-century Byzantine ceramic hand grenade used to spread "Greek fire," a sticky and highly flammable substance. The recipe for it has been lost to time; only empty grenades like these still exist.

SKELETON LAKE

Roopkund Lake, a.k.a. Skeleton Lake, in the Indian Himalayas is filled with bones from as many as 500 human skeletons. They were first discovered in 1942 at an altitude of about 16,000 ft (5,000 m), when a park ranger stumbled across hundreds of skeletons with swollen flesh still clinging to their bones. Nobody knows how the bodies got there, but some studies suggest they perished in a disaster around 1,200 years ago.

HANGOVER MUSEUM

In December 2019, Rino Dubokovic, a student in Zagreb, Croatia, opened the Museum of the Hangover, chronicling unusual hangover stories and displaying objects relating to hangover experiences. The aim of the project is to make visitors aware of the dangers of alcohol.

ULTRA MARATHON

Big's Backyard Ultra in Bell Buckle, Tennessee, is a marathon race consisting of a 4.1-mi (6.6-km) loop that is run continuously day and night until there is only one competitor left. The 2019 winner, Maggie Guterl, from Durango, Colorado, ran for a grueling 60 hours—two and a half days—and completed 250 mi (400 km).

VIKING CROSSINGS

To celebrate its Viking heritage, the Danish city of Aarhus recently replaced 17 traditional crosswalk signal light figures with images of Viking warriors holding axes and shields.

UNDISCOVERED ISLAND

Although Madagascar, located 250 mi (400 km) off the southeast coast of Africa, is the world's fourth-largest island, it took humans 300,000 years to discover it. It is thought the island was only colonized around 500 AD—300 millennia after the first appearance of *Homo sapiens* in nearby Africa.

HOTEL OLYMPICS

At the annual Las Vegas Housekeeping Olympics, teams of hotel workers compete in events such as bed-making races, vacuuming races, the mop relay, and the toilet paper toss.

HIGH FASHION

A fashion show was staged on January 26, 2020, at an altitude of 17,515 ft (5,340 m) in the Himalayas. The Mount Everest Fashion Runway was set up at Kala Patthar, Nepal, near the Everest base camp and included fashion models from all over the world wearing clothing made from yak wool.

POOP GIN

South Africa's Indlovu Gin is infused with elephant dung. Creators Les and Paula Ansley collect the dung themselves. It is dried and sterilized before use, and five large bags of elephant poop make up to 4,000 bottles of gin. The Ansleys had the idea after learning that elephants eat a lot of fruits and flowers but digest less than a third of them.

WASTED BEER

More than 160,000 pints of Guinness stout are wasted annually due to being trapped in drinkers' mustaches.

GREAT MOSQUE

The Great Mosque of Mecca in Saudi Arabia can accommodate more than 1.5 million people at once. During the 2019 Hajj, when millions of worshippers visit Mecca, the mosque closed its doors at 9 a.m. for their Friday prayers because it was full to capacity, despite prayers not starting until 12:30 p.m.

LOST ISLAND

Norway-owned Bouvet Island in the South Atlantic Ocean is 1,400 mi (2,250 km) from the nearest inhabited land. It is so remote that after being discovered in 1739, it was lost again for another 69 years.

FALL FASHION

Four Chinese fashion designers created a red carpet–ready look using 5,888 leaves. They gathered the leaves at the Shampoola scenic area in China's Guangdong Province. Their goal for the stunning floor-length dress with train was to raise awareness of environmental issues facing the region. Style has come a long way since those paltry single fig leaves in the Garden of Eden!

MUD RUN

At the annual Paantu Punaha festival on Miyako Island in Okinawa, Japan, three men covered in muddy vines and wearing masks smear onlookers, buildings, and cars with ink-colored mud to scare away evil spirits and attract good luck.

The mud represents a form of exorcism, and the muddy, foliage-covered *paantu* personify supernatural beings. Their ultimate goal? To get mud on everybody and everything. Not a festival for the faint of heart, onlookers should come prepared to get dirty. During past festivals, tidy tourists offended at getting covered in mud have attacked paantu. To avoid over-tourism and unwanted confrontations, organizers announce festival dates last minute, and paantu enlist attendants to protect them.

CURSE OF THE MUMMY

This monument on the Austrian-Italian border marks where Ötzi was found in 1991.

A shocking amount of people related to the finding of the famous Ötzi the Iceman mummy have died early deaths, leading some to believe the corpse is cursed.

Rainer Henn, the head of the forensic team examining the 5,000-year-old mummified corpse, died in a car crash in 1992 on his way to give a lecture about Ötzi and was just one of seven premature deaths connected to the Iceman. Not long after, Kurt Fritz, the mountaineer who led Henn to Ötzi's body, died in an avalanche (the only one of his party to be hit). A few months after Fritz's passing, the only man who filmed Ötzi's removal from the mountain, Austrian journalist Rainer Hoelzl, died at age 47 of a brain tumor.

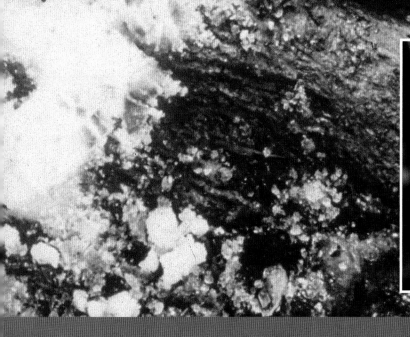

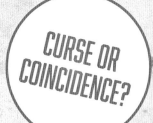

Ötzi is so well-preserved that his tattoos remain clearly visible, despite being thousands of years old!

Erika and Helmut Simon discovered Ötzi while hiking. Helmut was found dead near the same spot 13 years later.

Perhaps the creepiest death of all was that of Helmut Simon, one of the German tourists who found Ötzi on the Austrian-Italian border in 1991—he was also found dead frozen in ice near the same spot in 2004. He had fallen to his death during a freak blizzard. Within an hour of Simon's funeral, Dieter Warnecke, the head of the mountain rescue team sent to find him, died of a heart attack.

Then, archaeologist Konrad Spindler, who first inspected Ötzi's corpse, died of complications from multiple sclerosis in 2005. And California-born biologist Dr. Tom Loy, who carried out DNA analysis on Ötzi's corpse and had almost finished writing a book about him, died suddenly in 2005 aged 63.

When presented in this way, it definitely seems like involving yourself with Ötzi might curse you to die prematurely. But the truth is, it's easy to create patterns when you are looking for them. Many other scientists, journalists, photographers, and others have studied Ötzi and gone on to live full lives.

ARTICHOKE RACKET

In 1935, New York City mayor Fiorello LaGuardia tackled the Mafia by banning artichokes. Artichoke racketeering had become widespread across the United States, spearheaded by Sicilian-born underworld boss Ciro Terranova, with kidnapping, extortion, and murder all linked to sales of the vegetable. Public outrage at not being able to buy artichokes meant that LaGuardia's ban was lifted within a week, but criminal investigations soon brought an end to Terranova's racket.

SEWAGE ORDEAL

A woman in Clackamas County, Oregon, survived despite being trapped for three days in a septic tank at her home after accidentally falling into a 3-ft-deep (0.9-m) sewage hole. She was eventually found lying with her face just above the raw sewage.

STUDENT SYNDROME

Intern's syndrome is a condition commonly reported among medical students, who fear they may have the very disease that they are studying.

NO HEARTBEAT

While hiking in Spain in freezing weather in November 2019, a British woman, Audrey Mash, survived six hours without a heartbeat. Her body fell into hypothermia so quickly that her organs were preserved until she was resuscitated by doctors in Barcelona.

PUNCH IT

Retired teacher Peter Duffell has spent the past 50 years (and a small fortune) collecting hole punches from all over the world. The pieces in his collection date from the early 1800s through the 1960s. Yet he was in for a disappointment when he decided to auction off the collection at his wife's bidding. While he paid upward of £800 for some individual pieces, the whole collection hit the auction block for a measly £200.

HOMER'S VOICE

Homer Simpson is one of the most downloaded GPS voices in the world.

AMERICAN SOIL

George Washington once vowed that he would never set foot on English soil again. Therefore, in the 1920s, when the state of Virginia gifted a statue of Washington to the UK, they added some American soil to go beneath the plinth in London's Trafalgar Square so that his wish could be honored.

SLOW START

Former Formula 1 world champion Jenson Button failed his first driver's test. He was 17 when he took the test in Wiltshire, England, but failed because he drove too close to a parked car.

SWEATY ROBOT

Researchers at Cornell University engineered a 3D-printed robot "muscle" that can sweat like a human. When the temperature gets too hot, cooling water is squeezed out of the robotic hand's synthetic pores, making the robot sweat. It is hoped the technique will stop robots from malfunctioning because of overheating.

LITTLE FINGER

If you were ever to have your pinky finger removed, you would lose about half the strength in that hand.

PIECE OF CAKE

Self-taught Ukrainian baker Kristina Dolnyk creates cakes that look as though she has taken a slice right out of the ocean! A clever combination of cake, chocolate sculptures, and blue gelatin results in a one-of-a-kind dessert that not only looks amazing but tastes great, too! Dolnyk spends up to three days creating her hyperrealistic cakes and spends the rest of her time teaching others how to achieve similar effects.

WET BLANKET

A female blanket octopus can weigh up to 40,000 times more than her male counterpart!

While the males only get to be about the size of a walnut, the females can grow more than 6 ft (1.8 m) long! Their name comes from the thin piece of skin between their arms. When threatened, the blanket octopus can drop the webbing as a distraction, much like how a lizard will drop its tail when attacked. But when they're on the hunt, blanket octopuses have a secret weapon up their iridescent sleeves! They are immune to the painful sting of a Portuguese man-of-war, and will rip the tentacles off the creature and use them to stun prey.

RAD PAD

These extravagantly sized lily pads are so big they can hold the weight of a human being!

Native to South America, the leaves of the giant water lily (*Victoria amazonica*) measure between 4 to 6 ft (1.2 to 1.8 m) in diameter. One plant can produce up to 50 pads in a single season. And the pads aren't the only impressive part of giant water lilies—their flowers are special, too! They bloom for just two nights: the first night, the blossom is white and produces heat and scents to attract beetles, which get trapped inside the flower until the second night, when the flower opens up with pink petals, allowing the beetles to escape and spread the plant's pollen.

ANCIENT STEW

Guests at a 1984 dinner party at the Alaska home of paleontologist Dale Guthrie were served a stew containing meat from a 50,000-year-old bison. The remains of the ancient bison (named Blue Babe) had been discovered five years earlier buried in ice near Fairbanks and were well preserved, having been frozen for so many centuries. So Guthrie cut off a small part of the neck, thawed it, and served it with vegetables to his eight guests.

BUSY AIRPORT

The remote Canadian outpost city of Gander on Newfoundland used to be home to the world's largest airport, with four runways. In the 1940s and 1950s, before the jet age, airplanes used Gander as an essential refueling stop on transatlantic flights.

CONVICT TRAMWAY

Australia's first passenger railway was a 5-mi-long (8-km) tramway operated by prisoners at the nearby Port Arthur penitentiary in Tasmania. The tramway opened in 1836 with four-wheeled open carts pushed manually along the wooden rails by convicts.

TAP WINE

A fault at a nearby winery caused taps in homes in the Italian village of Settecani to dispense red wine instead of water on March 4, 2020. The fault had caused the wine to leak from a silo into the water pipes.

SENATE SOUP

The U.S. Senate restaurant has served bean soup every day, from the same recipe, for more than 100 years—except on September 14, 1943. On that day, World War II rationing left the Senate kitchen without enough navy beans to make the soup.

PUBLICITY STUNT

The town of Hot Springs, New Mexico, permanently changed its name to Truth or Consequences in March 1950 after Ralph Edwards, host of the radio show *Truth or Consequences*, announced that he would air the program on its tenth anniversary from the first town to rename itself after the show.

TINY ISLAND

Just Enough Room Island—part of the Thousand Islands archipelago on the St. Lawrence River between the United States and Canada—covers an area of around 3,300 sq ft (306 sq m), making it the world's smallest inhabited island. It is owned by the Sizeland family, who changed its name from Hub Island because there is just enough room for their house, a couple of trees, and a tiny beach.

FANFEED

FITTING NAME

This submission comes to us from Derek Beeman, a third-generation "bee man." In 1946, Derek's grandfather, Henry, appeared in a Ripley's Believe It or Not! cartoon drawn by Robert Ripley as the first beekeeper in the Beeman family. Today, Derek enthusiastically continues the honey-producing family tradition in Millville, California.

STONE SEA

In Pennsylvania's Poconos Mountains, you'll find a real anomaly: an 18-acre bed of rocks smackdab in the middle of a forest. Designated a national landmark in 1967, the rocks at Hickory Run Boulder Field range from less than 1.5 ft (45 cm) to more than 25 ft (7.6 m) long. The tops of the stones are all about the same level. One theory claims the rocky field developed during the last ice age, between 15,000 and 20,000 years ago, but the mechanisms behind the process remain largely unknown.

SKIJORING

Skijoring is the winter sport of skiing while being pulled by dogs or horses!

The name comes from the Norwegian word *skikjøring*, which means "ski driving." While in both versions of the sport a skier is attached to one or more animals with the help of a harness, there are key differences. When it comes to equine skijoring, the horse does most of the pulling and may also have a rider. Horse skijoring courses can include jumps, ramps, and ring catches. But when skijoring with a dog, the skier helps propel themselves along with their poles, and race courses are mainly trail-based. Dogs weighing as little as 30 lb (14 kg) can participate in skijoring, as long as they are properly trained.

SAWN IN HALF

English singer Paloma Faith once worked as a magician's assistant called Miss Direction in an act where she was sawn in half every night. She was also levitated and often shared a box with a live rabbit. She also previously worked as a ghost on a theme park ride.

COMPLEX COSTUME

Willem Dafoe's Green Goblin costume for the 2002 movie *Spider-Man* was composed of 580 pieces and took him at least a half an hour to put on.

FORTNITE BET

Students at Tippecanoe High School, Tipp City, Ohio, made a bet with their chemistry teacher, Mike McCray, that if their tweet challenge received 6,700 retweets, he would agree to change their final exam to include questions related to the video game *Fortnite*. They won the bet, as their tweet was retweeted more than 30,000 times.

RECLUSIVE AUTHOR

After the success of his first novel, *The Catcher in the Rye*, J. D. Salinger spent 50 years living as a recluse in Cornish, New Hampshire, and his agent had orders to burn all fan mail.

PAINT BOX

Nicknamed the "Preschool Picasso," seven-year-old Mikail Akar, from Cologne, Germany, creates abstract pictures by punching paint onto the canvas while wearing his father's boxing gloves. He started painting at age four, and his works have sold for more than $12,000 USD.

KITCHEN MASTERPIECE

Christ Mocked, a long-lost painting by thirteenth-century Italian artist Cimabue, sold for $26.6 million USD at auction in October 2019—a few months after being found hanging above a hot plate in the kitchen of an elderly French woman's home in Compiègne.

HORROR SCHOOL

The Miskatonic Institute of Horror Studies runs courses in Montreal, New York City, Los Angeles, and London, teaching topics like zombies in horror films, reality horror, and horror.

VANISHING ORCHESTRA

First performed in 1772, the "Farewell Symphony" by Austrian composer Joseph Haydn requires all of the musicians to leave the stage one by one until only two violins are left playing at the end.

PAPER PIANO

When his family was unable to afford to buy him a real piano, 11-year-old Andrew Garrido, from London, England, created his own paper keyboard so he could practice. He researched the dimensions of a keyboard, drew the keys on a piece of paper, and stuck it to his desk. It helped him through his first five piano grades with distinction, and he has since gone on to play a real piano at concert venues across Europe.

PILOT LICENSE

Morgan Freeman got his pilot license at age 65. He had been a mechanic in the U.S. Air Force in his late teens and had considered training as a fighter pilot, but his acting career eventually took priority.

'80s CALLBACK

If you've ever felt like you were born in the wrong decade, look no further than the *Bill and Ted's Excellent Adventure* Phone Booth!

The iconic time-traveling machine was officially licensed and recreated by custom phone booth manufacturer Cubicall as a throwback to the 1989 film *Bill and Ted's Excellent Adventure*. The limited-run design is retrofitted for VOIP/landline services and includes an umbrella-travel antenna, but no word yet on its time-traveling capabilities.

CARTOON CARPENTRY

Equal parts fantastical and functional, Henk Verhoeff's furniture looks like it was pulled straight from the pages of a storybook.

The New Zealand woodworker has been making cabinets for more than 50 years and has put all of that experience to the test with these distorted dressers. Some of his pieces even incorporate lighting, giving them a magical glow. Despite their irregular, chaotic, and even broken appearances, customers are delighted to find each unique piece fully functional.

SIX-STORY FALL

Winston, a two-year-old French bulldog, survived a six-story fall from the roof of a Manhattan building because he crashed through the sunroof of a parked car. Rushing to the scene, owner Emma Heinrich feared the worst but found him sitting in the driver's seat with only a few cuts and scratches.

ELEPHANT GUEST

A wild elephant named Natta Kota is a regular visitor to the Jetwing Yala Hotel in Sri Lanka, where he wanders around the lobby investigating furnishings and lamps with his trunk. The hotel complex is not fenced off from surrounding scrubland, meaning that wild animals are free to enter the grounds.

SNIFFER DOG

Following an argument with his wife, a man in Birmingham, England, angrily threw his wedding ring, but immediately regretted his actions and started frantically searching for the gold band in tall grass by the side of a road at two o'clock in the morning. He was spotted by police officer Carl Woodall with his police dog Odin, and in less than two minutes, the six-year-old German shepherd had sniffed out the small ring in the dark.

VEGAS SWARM

Following a wet spring, millions of grasshoppers descended on Las Vegas in July 2019, attracted to the bright lights. The insects blanketed sidewalks and streets in a swarm so large that it showed up on weather radar.

CAN PICTURE

Monica Mathis, of St. Paul, Minnesota, was reunited with her dog Hazel thanks to a beer company promotion. After Motorworks Brewing teamed up with Florida's Manatee County Animal Shelter and put shelter dogs' faces on their beer cans to encourage adoption, Mathis recognized one of the photos as her terrier mix that had gone missing three years earlier. Even though Hazel had a different name on the can, Mathis was able to provide pictures and vet records to prove that the dog was hers.

BEER BIRDS

The Royal Society for the Prevention of Cruelty to Animals (RSPCA) received dozens of calls regarding seagulls in Bournemouth, England, in the summer of 2018. The birds had been stumbling around drunk after drinking waste from local breweries.

CLIFF FALL

Archie, a four-year-old terrier, survived unhurt after plunging 100 ft (30 m) off a cliff on the Isle of Wight, England, while chasing a bird. He landed on a ledge that was so inaccessible from land he had to be rescued from the sea by lifeboat.

YOU ZOO

Roles are reversed at the Glen Garriff Conservation sanctuary in Harrismith, South Africa, where the visitors are in cages and lions are free to roam around! From the safety of an acrylic booth, up to two people at a time can get up close to rescued lions. Just like a house cat, these big cats love boxes and will lick, rub, and even jump on top of the cage. Small holes in the cage allow visitors to get crystal clear pictures of the majestic creatures.

LAST MEAL

A frog and spider left a grisly scene on the wall of Christine Watts's home in Myakka City, Florida. Four hairy legs protrude from the mummified amphibian's mouth, leaving the nearly 75,000 people who shared the image online wondering what in the world happened. Did the frog choke on the spider? Was the frog already dead when the spider decided to make a home inside the mouth? Or something else? Whatever happened is a mystery, but Watts confirms that both creatures were dead when she found them. She even kept the mummies!

CURLY FLIES

The frillback pigeon looks like it's fresh out of the salon with a brand-new perm!

It has curly feathers on its wings, legs, and feet, while the rest of its feathers have a distinctive wave to them. The breed is popular at pigeon beauty contests—yes, you read that correctly—and its calm demeanor also makes it a good pet. And believe it or not, these birds can fly just fine.

LET'S PLAY

While video games were once considered a niche interest, they have steadily risen in popularity around the world and are now enjoyed by people from all walks of life. From joysticks to virtual reality goggles, here are some strange facts from video game history.

◄ 1 Virtual Success

Aerosmith has earned more money from the video game *Guitar Hero* than from any of their albums.

2 How to Win

By the end of 1985, the best-selling book in Japan was a strategy guide on how to beat the *Super Mario Bros.* game.

3 Among the Stars

Tetris was the first video game played in space.

5 Smell the Game

The PlayStation games *FIFA 2001* and *Gran Turismo 2* had scratch-and-sniff discs that smelled like a soccer field and car tires, respectively.

6 M for Money

Grand Theft Auto V has made more money than any movie ever!

4 Early Start

Nintendo originally sold playing cards.

7 In Control

The PlayStation 1 controller was 10% larger in the U.S. compared to Japan to compensate for Americans' larger hands.

CREWMATE CHECKMATE

Jessica Zhang of Orange, California, crafted this *Among Us*–themed chess set!

Using polymer clay and paint, Zhang transformed the popular video game's two-dimensional avatars into three-dimensional chess pieces. Using different colors and silly hats, she was able to differentiate the queen, king, rooks, bishops, and knights from each other. The pawns are perfectly executed recreations of the game's dead bodies. And just like a normal chess set is divided into red or black and white players, these opposing pieces can be told apart by their colored bases.

TrainStation

On November 17, 2020, London Underground commuters did a double-take as new roundel signs featuring classic PlayStation controller buttons greeted them. The sign switch occurred at the Oxford Circus tube station entrances, where gamer twists transformed the tube's classic red circle symbol into blue Xs, pink squares, and green triangles. The playful swap was orchestrated by Sony to promote the release of PlayStation 5.

Ripley's Exhibit
Cat. No. 168338

JACK NICHOLSON BOOK CARVING

Artist Alex Queral of Philadelphia, Pennsylvania, carves portraits out of telephone books! There are several in Ripley's collection, including this one of actor Jack Nicholson, known for his portrayal of Jack Torrance in the 1980 adaptation of Stephen King's *The Shining*, among other roles.

Ripley's Exhibit
Cat. No. 165965

STEPHEN KING LIFE MASK

A casting of Stephen King's face. The undisputed master of horror, King has published more than 60 novels and hundreds of short stories. Much of his work has been adapted into movies and TV series, such as *Carrie*, *IT*, *Pet Sematary*, and more.

EDGAR ALLAN POE SMOKE PORTRAIT

Daniel Diehl of Charleston, South Carolina, created this version of nineteenth-century poet and writer Edgar Allan Poe by passing his canvas through the smoke of a candle. Diehl's "In a Puff of Smoke" series celebrates historic figures who died young and unexpectedly.

EDGAR ALLAN POE

Edgar Allan Poe is a name that conjures up daydreams of the dreadful, thoughts of graveyards and goblins, ravens, and writing desks, in many cases.

Even though his story is often shrouded in mystery and punched up for tragedy, in reality, Poe's life saw the mundane about as often as the macabre. In honor of the woeful writer, here are some strange facts about Poe that his legend doesn't usually tend to shine a light on.

Literature Linebackers

Poe spent many of his years living in Baltimore, Maryland. He was also eventually laid to rest there for good. And in 1996, when the city's new professional football team needed a name, fans were asked to weigh in on the big decision. Surveys indicated that two-thirds of the more than 33,000 individuals who voted opted to name the team the Baltimore Ravens, in honor of Poe's most famous poem.

Paltry Pay

Many people see Edgar Allan Poe as the quintessential penniless writer, and that's not far off the mark. His fiction hardly ever amounted to much financially. He made $9 for "The Raven" and just over $50 for "The Murders in the Rue Morgue." To supplement his income, he wrote for the *Southern Literary Messenger* and was quite a fearsome critic in his day. However, Poe's best-selling book during his lifetime was *The Conchologist's First Book*, a textbook about seashells!

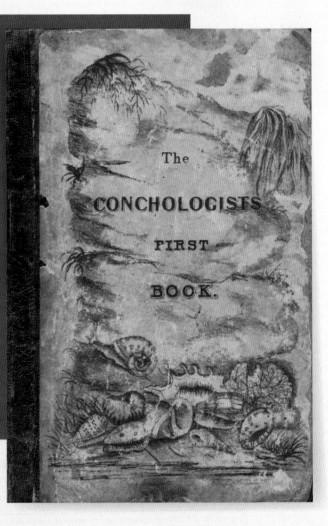

Identity Mystery

Published in 1842, "The Masque of the Red Death" is one of Poe's most famous short stories. It's about a prince who throws a masquerade ball for the wealthy and elite, all while his subjects suffer from a deadly disease outside his walls. In the end, the disease itself shows up at the masquerade and wipes out everyone inside. Some scholars believe this was a story inspired by tuberculosis, which took the lives of Poe's wife, mother, brother, and foster mother. Others say the plague was meant to mirror the cholera epidemic he witnessed in Baltimore. Either way, Poe himself expressed that he did not care for literature that sought to instruct or provide a moral, making it hard to determine what, if anything, he was attempting to say in the tale.

Quoth the Parrot

"The Raven" is often considered to be Poe's most widely known work. However, the poem might have fallen a bit flat had Poe gone with his original idea: a parrot. In his 1846 essay "The Philosophy of Composition," Poe wrote that "very naturally, a parrot, in the first instance, suggested itself" as the prophecy-spouting specter-bird, but the author quickly became concerned about the creature's vibrant nature not being in line with the tone of the piece. Therefore, it "was superseded forthwith by a Raven as equally capable of speech, and infinitely more in keeping with the intended tone."

Cooped Up

On October 3, 1849, Poe was found on the street, ranting and incomprehensible—and dressed in someone else's clothing. He died days later, and although drunkenness could explain the odd behavior, the doctor who attended Poe said he "had not the slightest odor of liquor upon his breath or person." Rabies, seizures, and a brain tumor have all been suggested as causes of death.

Another possible explanation is a form of voter fraud at the time known as "cooping." People were kidnapped and drugged, often dressed in different clothes, then forced to vote multiple times for a particular candidate. Still, no conclusive proof about the cause of Poe's death has ever surfaced.

Unmarked Grave

For the first 26 years after Poe's death, he was buried in Baltimore's Westminster Hall and Burying Ground without a headstone. This was not solely because of his financial woes, as many believe, but actually because the headstone that was created for him was destroyed in a freak accident where a train went off the tracks and smashed it to bits! In 1875, he was finally reburied and given a proper monument in honor of his literary contributions.

ORIGINAL BURIAL PLACE OF
EDGAR ALLAN POE
FROM
OCTOBER 9, 1849,
UNTIL
NOVEMBER 17, 1875.

MRS. MARIA CLEMM, HIS MOTHER-IN-LAW, LIES UPON HIS RIGHT AND VIRGINIA POE, HIS WIFE, UPON HIS LEFT, UNDER THE MONUMENT ERECTED TO HIM IN THIS CEMETERY.

PURPLE PROBLEM

The amethyst appearance of Paraguay's Cerro Lagoon in Limpio hides a deadly secret—lethal pollution. Residents first noticed the lagoon's changing color in mid-2020 after the completion of an embankment and roadway splitting the waterway in half. One side remains healthy and "normal" looking. The other has grown increasingly plum-colored, smelly, and filled with flies attracted to massive die-offs of fish and herons. What's causing the livid, lavender waters? Chromium pollution from a nearby leather tanning factory.

AIRPLANE FOOD
Budget airline AirAsia runs a chain of restaurants on the ground that sell airplane food in cardboard boxes. The first, Santan, opened in a mall in Kuala Lumpur, Malaysia, and the airplane dishes on its menu cost around $3 each.

TUMBLEWEED MOUNTAIN
State Route 240 near West Richland, Washington, was closed for 10 hours on New Year's Day 2020 after cars were trapped by piles of tumbleweed up to 30 ft (9 m) high.

MONSTER FATBERG
A fatberg found in a sewer in Sidmouth, Devon, England, measured 210 ft (64 m) long, making it bigger than the Leaning Tower of Pisa. In addition to waste and grease, the giant fatberg contained a pair of false teeth.

CHILDREN'S RAILWAY
The approximately 7-mi-long (11-km) Children's Railway, near Budapest, Hungary, is a tourist line run almost entirely by children. Only the driver and a few supervisors are adults. The rest of the staff are children aged between 10 and 14 who must achieve good grades and pass railway exams to be selected.

RANDOM LETTERS
The town of Ixonia, Wisconsin, got its name in 1846 by drawing random letters out of a hat until a word could be formed. The letters of the alphabet were written on slips of paper and were drawn from the bag by a young girl named Mary Piper.

BEAN DIP
For Super Bowl LIV in 2020, Bush's Beans made a 70-layer bean dip weighing 1,087 lb (493 kg). It took 19 people around 227 hours to assemble the gargantuan snack, which featured 10 varieties of seven-layer dip stacked atop one another.

LONG JOB
It is expected to take 13 years to paint the nearly 5-mi-long (8-km) Øresund Bridge, which links Denmark and Sweden.

WICKED WITCH
At Christmas in the Bavaria region of Germany, children are traditionally visited by a witch named Perchta to see if they have been naughty or well-behaved during the year. If they have been bad, legend says she disembowels them and fills their bodies with straw and stones.

SNOW WAY!

Each year, the Bartz brothers of Minnesota sculpt an enormous animal using hundreds of thousands of pounds of snow!

Austin, Trevor, and Connor Bartz started sculpting masterpieces out of snow in 2012. Their pride and joy, "Walvis the Whale," required 260,000 lb (118,000 kg) of snow and 600 hours to complete. Walvis invited locals to snap selfies and pics, and even had special effects like blue steam billowing from his blowhole. The brothers asked visitors of the fishy creation to donate $25, with proceeds helping provide clean water for people in Uganda and Niger.

SILENT AUDIENCE

On June 22, 2020, the Gran Teatre del Liceu in Barcelona, Spain, held concert for 2,292 plants

The show was in honor of health care professionals who had been working during the COVID-19 crisis and a way to kick off the theater's 2020–2021 season. The greenery was treated to a string quartet performance of Puccini's "Crisantemi," a late-nineteenth-century piece inspired by chrysanthemum flowers. After the concert, the plants were gifted to health care workers.

FLARE UP

Daredevil Kyle Marquart made headlines after purposely incinerating his parachute using a flare gun at 7,000 ft (2,134 m). Known as a "canopy burn," Marquart relied on an old reserve in a "tertiary setup" to survive the brush with self-imposed disaster. In other words, he packed three parachutes during the stunt over Austin, Texas, relying on the latter two once his initial parachute burned out.

DIFFERENT DAYS
The Russian island of Big Diomede and the Alaskan island of Little Diomede in the Bering Strait are only 2.4 mi (3.8 km) apart, but because they are separated by the International Date Line, they are also 21 hours apart. From Little Diomede, it is technically possible to see the next day on Big Diomede.

SHORT JOURNEY
Each year, tourists spend around £105,000 on London Underground journeys between Covent Garden and Leicester Square, even though the two stations are less than 900 ft (274 m) apart. The train journey takes just 45 seconds.

DIFFERENT LIGHTS
Even though Berlin, Germany, has been united since the fall of the Berlin Wall in 1989, from space it is still possible to distinguish the east and west sides of the city because the street lights in the east still use yellow sodium but in the west they are white.

DIAMOND RAIN
It rains diamonds on Saturn. Lightning storms turn the methane gas in the planet's atmosphere into soot (carbon), which hardens into graphite and then diamonds as it falls. An estimated 1,100 tons of diamonds, each about 0.4 in (1 cm) in diameter, are created on Saturn every year.

SKULL TOWER
A tower in Niš, Serbia, displays around 50 human skulls. It was constructed following a war between the Serbians and the Ottomans in the early nineteenth century when the heads of the defeated Serbian rebels were ordered to be skinned, stuffed, and sent to the Ottoman sultan, Mahmud II. The sultan then had the skulls returned to Niš with the instruction that a tower be built and the skulls displayed as a warning to any future rebels. When finished, the Skull Tower stood 15 ft (4.6 m) high and had 952 skulls embedded in its sides. Over the years, many have been removed by relatives of the deceased or by souvenir hunters.

DIVIDING LINE
The border between France and Switzerland runs right through the bed in the honeymoon suite at the Hotel Arbez in the villages of La Cure, France, and Les Rousses, Switzerland.

CUCUMBER CURE
Instead of putting salt on their roads in winter to prevent ice from forming, authorities in the German region of Bavaria have experimented with using leftover pickled cucumber juice.

FUNERAL FONDUE
Residents of Grimentz, Switzerland, used to spend years aging wheels of cheese just so that it could be eaten at their own funerals.

TOBOGGAN DRIFTING

The Monte Sledge—a wicker toboggan—served as a form of public transportation in Funchal, Madeira, Portugal, in the 1850s and continues to offer hair-raising rides today.

The "Carro de Cesto" flies from the Nossa Senhora do Monte Church down a winding road to the suburb of Livramento, both terrifying and transporting tourists. Two "Carreiros" dressed in white with straw hats and rubber-soled shoes steer and stop the street sled. The toboggan itself is a big wicker basket with two wooden runners wrapped in greased rags. The 10-minute, 1.24-mi (2 km) ride reaches speeds of 30 mph (48.3 kmph) and will make you a believer in traveler's insurance.

BLIND CLIMBER
Jesse Dufton, from Leicestershire, England, led a climbing team up the challenging 450-ft-high (137-m) vertical rock known as the Old Man of Hoy on the Orkney Islands, Scotland, even though he is blind.

LIFE LOGGER
Morris Villarroel, a Spanish scientist at the Polytechnic University of Madrid, has written down every single thing he has done since 2010. He keeps a detailed record of every aspect of his life—no matter how mundane—making notes every 15 to 30 minutes during the day. His experiences, which include the places he was in at the time and the people he met, take up more than 300 logbooks.

SKYDIVING BROTHERS
In 2019, Elliot Shimmin from the UK completed 19 somersaults in a single skydive over Lake Elsinore, California. Two years earlier, his younger brother Harry had managed 19 backward somersaults in a skydive over Cambridgeshire, England, before deploying his parachute.

NOODLE HOUSE
Mr. Zhang, from Jilin Province, China, spent four days building a playhouse for his son from 2,000 packets of expired instant noodles, all fixed together with glue. The noodle cabin measures about 43 sq ft (4 sq m) and is big enough to accommodate a bed, windows, and even some artwork!

EVERY STREET
Computer programmer Davis Vilums spent five years cycling along every street in the center of London. He moved to England from his native Latvia in 2012 and completed most of the challenge on his way to work, tracking his progress with a GPS and highlighting his routes on A to Z maps of the capital.

REAL-LIFE CYBORG
Ben Workman, of Springville, Utah, has four computer chips embedded in his hands that allow him to perform different functions—lock and unlock his car, open doors at his workplace, log into his computer, and share contact information—just by waving his hand nearby. He also has a magnet implanted under the skin in his left hand so that he can play tricks and amuse his friends.

MILLION MILES
Eighty-two-year-old Russ Mantle, from Surrey, England, has cycled 1 million mi (1.6 million km)—the equivalent of circling the equator 40 times. He has kept detailed records of every bike ride he has done since the 1950s.

Students at Bullock Creek High School in Midland, Michigan, spent 16 hours building a 16-ft-tall (5-m) pyramid from 27,434 rolls of toilet paper.

LADY IN RED

For 50 years, nearly everything that Zorica Rebernik owns has been a shade of red, from her house in Breze, Bosnia, to her hair, clothes, kitchen utensils, and furniture.

The obsession began when she was around 18 years old, when she had a "sudden, strong urge to wear red." Rebernik says the vibrant hue makes her feel strong and powerful. She uses red kitchen appliances, was married in a red gown, and even has a tombstone made with red granite prepared for when she dies!

EXTRA DIGITS

Kumar Nayak of Ganjam, India, was born with 20 toes and 12 fingers, a condition known as polydactyly. The condition is relatively common; however, it usually results in just one extra digit, making Nayak's case extremely rare.

HUMAN FACE

In January 2020, a one-of-a-kind goat owned by Mukeshji Prajapap was born in Rajasthan, India, with a flat, human-like face, prompting villagers to worship the animal as a divine figure. The goat was born with a rare congenital defect called *cyclopia*, which affects the genes that create facial characteristics.

FACTORY HABITAT

The rare spring pygmy sunfish has twice been declared extinct but lives on near a huge automobile factory in Huntsville, Alabama—one of only two places in the world where it can still be found.

TURNED WHITE

The black coat of Blaze, a 10-year-old Labrador retriever from Suomi, Finland, turned white over the course of a year due to vitiligo, a skin condition that results in a loss of natural pigmentation. It started with a small white patch on his ear but soon spread to his face and torso.

VOLCANO HOME

Alaskan fur seals regularly breed on Bogoslof Island, located north of the Aleutian Islands, even though it is the summit of an active undersea volcano that constantly releases hot steam and volcanic gases, as well as boiling mud geysers up to 16 ft (5 m) tall.

FAN FEED

LAP OF LUXURY

London couple Rebecca and Alex May shared with us a fake lap they made for their cat! Ziggy loves cuddling with her humans and would go to any length to be near them, including sitting on their shoulders or loudly meowing until she is given attention. Rebecca and Alex were happy that the adoptive feline felt comfortable around them, but it was beginning to interfere with their jobs since they worked from home. So, Alex stuffed a pair of his pants with a duvet cover, towel, and heating pad—and, remarkably, Ziggy took to it immediately! Now if they ever need personal space, they simply reassemble the surrogate lap.

BACHELOR PAD

The male satin bowerbird takes building a romantic relationship to the next level by crafting and decorating a bower to attract females. Males use parallel walls of sticks cemented with saliva and chewed vegetable matter to make these courtship arenas. To set the mood, males decorate their bowers with bright blue objects. Items include indigo clothes pins, cobalt bottle tops, and sapphire parrot feathers.

DADDY DEAREST

Believe it or not, male seahorses give birth!

In most species, the female is the one who carries the offspring until they are ready to face the world, but this isn't true for seahorses and their close relatives the pipefish and seadragon. In these cases, the female deposits her eggs into the male's brood pouch, where they are fertilized and form into miniature versions of their parents. When the babies are ready to be born, the male opens the brood pouch and a series of contractions forces the younglings out. Some seahorses give birth to more than 1,000 babies at a time!

SECRET CELEB SKILLS

You may recognize these names from the big screen, but their skills go beyond acting! Check out these surprising skills of your favorite celebs.

1 Mark Ruffalo

When Mark Ruffalo isn't busy "hulking" around with the Avengers, he excels at a sport that would make P.T. Barnum proud: unicycling.

2 Chloë Grace Moretz

American actress, Chloë Grace Moretz, proves no stranger to knife-wielding and has been practicing self-defense with a butterfly blade since the tender age of 11.

3 Patrick Dempsey

We all know Patrick Dempsey as *Grey's Anatomy*'s "McDreamy," but he has a hidden passion you've likely never heard of—pro race car driving.

4 Margot Robbie

Margot Robbie, everyone's favorite bad girl, dabbles in tattooing and has given nearly 100 permanent stamps, including one to fellow *Suicide Squad* star Cara Delevingne.

5 Conan O'Brien

When he's not busy entertaining late-night talk show fans, Conan O'Brien boasts impeccable tap-dancing skills.

6 Jennifer Garner

Hollywood A-lister Jennifer Garner can wail on the saxophone Lisa Simpson–style, and she's also a prodigious spoons player and clogger.

7 Steve Martin

If Jennifer Garner's ever looking for a bandmate, she should call Steve Martin, a banjo-picking maverick who tours regularly with his group The Steep Canyon Rangers.

8 Neil Patrick Harris

Neil Patrick Harris, known for his TV roles such as the devious Count Olaf in Netflix's *A Series of Unfortunate Events*, is also an award-winning magician.

HAIR THIN

Micro-artist Graham Short, from Birmingham, England, engraved a miniscule portrait onto a gold disc fitted inside a hollowed-out strand of dog hair.

Short recreated the likeness of nineteenth-century English artist J. M. W. Turner in recognition of the artist being featured on the £20 note. Using a microscope with a magnification of ×400, he spent 75 hours using ultra-fine needles to create the image within a 0.0039-in-thick (0.1-mm) sheepdog hair. To keep a steady hand, he took medication to lower his heart rate to around 25 beats a minute and worked between beats. The picture is so tiny it is invisible to the naked eye!

DRIVEWAY CANVAS

Diana Wood, from Burlington, North Carolina, uses a power washer to turn her concrete driveway into a canvas for pictures of birds, animals, plants, and butterflies. She uses it like a giant paint spray can, changing the angle of the tip to achieve different degrees of cleanliness on the dirt-covered surface and form beautifully detailed illustrations.

SHY PIANIST

Polish composer and pianist Frédéric Chopin was chronically shy and only performed around 30 public concerts in his lifetime. He insisted on playing the piano in the dark. He would put out any candles in the room, and even when playing at an event or a party, he would ask for the light in the room to be extinguished first.

TOP BANANA

An artwork by Italy's Maurizio Cattelan consisting of an ordinary banana duct-taped to a wall sold for $120,000 in Florida in 2019. To maintain the installation, the banana must be replaced every few days, but in any case, it was removed from display at Art Basel Miami Beach a week after it was installed, when performance artist David Datuna ate it.

BLOCKB&B

Believe it or not, there was a time before Netflix and streaming, when you had to leave your house if you wanted to watch a movie you didn't own! For many, that meant visiting a rental store like Blockbuster. For three nights in September 2020, nostalgic '90s kids could book a classic sleepover right inside the last-standing Blockbuster store that still rents movies, located in Bend, Oregon. The retro setup featured movie snacks, a pull-out couch, and beanbag chairs, plus "new releases" from the '90s.

FIELD OF LIGHT

Internationally acclaimed British artist Bruce Munro created this multi-acre art installation.

Aptly titled *Field of Light*, it showcases more than 58,000 stemmed spheres. The piece was inspired by Munro's experience in the Red Desert of Australia, where he witnessed plants blooming "under a blazing blanket of stars." Fiber optics powered by solar energy illuminate each lamp, creating subtle buds of morphing color. *Field of Light* has gone on display at nearly 20 different locations around the world.

PERFECT BALANCE

The works of Palestinian entertainer Mohammed al-Shenbari appear to defy gravity! He can find the precise balancing point of any particular object, allowing him to achieve the seemingly impossible, such as standing chairs on one leg, balancing gas canisters on top of a vertical wrench, and even posing a large TV on the rim of a glass soda bottle. When he first started, it would take him days to complete a sculpture. After just one year of practice, it only takes him a few minutes!

EMERGENCY LANDING

On only his third-ever flying lesson, student pilot Max Sylvester was forced to make an emergency landing in Perth, Western Australia, after his trainer, Robert Mollard, lost consciousness in the airplane cockpit. With just two hours of flight experience to his name, Sylvester had to fly solo for 50 minutes in order to make a safe landing.

WHEELCHAIR ODYSSEY

From May 10, 2006, to December 6, 2007, Chang-Hyun Choi of South Korea drove 17,398 mi (28,000 km) in his mouth-controlled motorized wheelchair. Chang, who has cerebral palsy and is paralyzed from the neck down, traveled at a maximum speed of 8 mph (13 kmph) across 35 countries in Europe and the Middle East.

HIGHEST PEAKS

Nirmal Purja from Nepal climbed the world's 14 highest peaks—each one over 26,000 ft (8,000 m) high—in only 189 days. The feat has taken other climbers at least eight years to achieve. He even managed to climb Everest, Lhotse, and Makalu (the highest, fourth-highest, and fifth-highest mountains in the world) consecutively in just 48 hours.

PROFESSOR POWER

Using only his bare hands, William Clark, a professor at Binghamton University, New York, bent seven metal railroad spikes in one minute. In 2018, he ripped 23 license plates in half in 60 seconds.

AERIAL YOGA

On September 7, 2019, seven slackline walkers from around the world crossed a rope stretched 1,148 ft (350 m) aboveground in Moscow, Russia—that's higher than the Eiffel Tower. The group made the daring 708-ft-long (216-m) walk on a line strung between two high-rise towers. The next day, one member, Germany's Friedrich Kühne, even balanced on one leg to perform acrobatic yoga moves partway across the line.

Appearing on the Filipino TV variety show *Eat Bulaga*, actor Paolo Ballesteros kept his eyes open without blinking for 1 hour 17 minutes 3 seconds.

WIFE CARRYING

Olivia and Jerome Roehm, from Newark, Delaware, won six cases of beer and $555 (five times Olivia's weight of 111 lb) by winning the 2019 North American Wife Carrying Championship in Newry, Maine. The 834-ft-long (254-m) course features two log hurdles and a pit of muddy water called the "widowmaker."

BANDAGE SHOES

Eleven-year-old Rhea Ballos won multiple gold medals at an inter-school sports event in Iloilo, the Philippines, despite not having proper running shoes. She won the 400 meters, 800 meters, and 1,500 meters by running in makeshift shoes constructed out of bandages on which a handwritten Nike logo was scrawled.

CRAY CRAY

More than one ton of crayfish was used to create a massive version of themselves for a banquet in Luoyang, China.

Thousands of tourists gathered to enjoy a meal of the freshwater crustaceans, a favorite in the region. They are so popular, in fact, that less than a day's drive away in the city of Qianjiang, you can find a massive, 50-ft-tall (15-m) statue in honor of the freshwater shellfish.

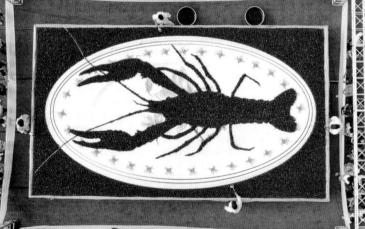

Ripley's Exhibit
Cat. No. 174286

APOLLO 11 MISSION ANALYZER

Astronauts Neil Armstrong, Buzz Aldrin, and Michael Collins used a chart like this to keep track of their schedule while on the first mission to the Moon.

Richard LeParmentar.
21 Sydney St. SW.3.

The
Adventures of Luke Starkiller
as taken from the
"Journal of the Whills"
by
George Lucas

(Saga I)
STAR WARS

Revised Fourth Draft
March 15, 1976

Lucasfilm Ltd.

Ripley's Exhibit
Cat. No. 174076

STAR WARS SCREENPLAY

One of the earliest drafts of the first *Star Wars* movie.
Luke Skywalker was originally named Luke Starkiller!

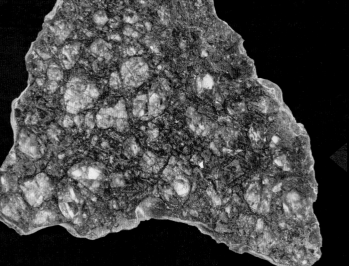

Ripley's Exhibit
Cat. No. 174086

PALLASITE METEORITE SLICE

Pallasite meteorites are filled with greenish-
gold crystals and are extremely rare. They
are one of the first types of rocks identified
as being extraterrestrial.

DARE TO FLY

Few Victorian performers delighted audiences and dominated newspaper headlines like aerialist Leona Dare (1855-1922) and her steel jaws.

Everything about Dare (born Susan Adeline Stuart) shocked and tantalized Victorian crowds, from her risqué costumes (featuring nude-colored body stockings) to her death-defying tricks. Employing a custom-made mouthpiece, she flew suspended from dizzying heights using nothing more than her jaws and teeth. Newspaper headlines lauded her as the "Comet of 1873," the "Queen of the Antilles," and the "Pride of Madrid." Soon, she incorporated male performer, M. George, into the show, holding the rope from which he hung between her clenched teeth—a stunt known today as the "Iron Jaw."

On December 13, 1884, disaster struck. Dare hung by her feet from the roof of a theater in Valencia, Spain. Clenched in her teeth were the ropes to a trapeze from which George hung. Suddenly seized by a "nervous fit," her jaws fell slack, and her partner plummeted to his death. She temporarily retired from the public eye, horrified by the terrible accident. By 1888, Dare was back at the top of her game, hanging suspended from a hot air balloon navigated by Eduard Spelterini. Reports claim the balloon would ascend upward of 5,000 ft (1,524 m) during her act. All told, Dare enjoyed an impressive career celebrated for her physical strength and stamina, two characteristics not typically admired in women of her day.

Modern circus artists performing the Iron Jaw.

Leona Dare's custom mouthpiece, seen here, is currently housed at the Northwest Museum of Arts & Culture in Spokane, Washington.

JUST ADD WATER

At the Thang Long Water Puppet Theater in Hanoi, Vietnam, puppeteers perform a show while standing waist deep in a 43-sq-ft (4-sq-m) tank of water!

The performers' presence is concealed from the audience by a split-bamboo screen. They then use long bamboo rods with string mechanisms, all hidden below the surface, to operate the wooden puppets, so that they appear to move across the water on their own. The tradition dates back to the eleventh century, when the rice fields flooded and villagers in the Red River Delta used to entertain each other with water puppetry.

CHEAP ROOM
In 2019, guests could stay in room 8 at the Asahi Ryokan Hotel in Fukuoka, Japan, for just $1 a night—but their entire stay was livestreamed on YouTube.

WOODEN POLES
The Royal Palace in Amsterdam, the Netherlands, sits on 13,659 wooden poles. The palace was built on swampy land from 1648 to 1665, and the poles are fixed into a sandy layer of soil more than 35 ft (11 m) below ground to stop the building from sinking.

TRUCK GARDENS
Every year, landscaping experts from Japan compete in the Kei Truck Garden Contest, where participants turn the flat beds of mini trucks into beautifully designed miniature gardens. Some of the gardens are so elaborate that they include aquariums and waterfalls.

UNIQUE TOWN
Saint-Louis-du-Ha! Ha! in Quebec, Canada, is the only town in the world with two exclamation points in its name.

AIRPLANE DELIVERY
Each week, Papa Murphy's pizza company in Anchorage flies hundreds of miles, delivering approximately 150 frozen pizzas to remote locations in Alaska via airplane. Orders are flown out as far as Prudhoe Bay, which would be a journey of 855 mi (1,368 km) by car.

FUNERAL POET
If someone in Amsterdam, the Netherlands, dies with no friends or family to prepare their funeral or mourn over their body, a poet will compose a poem and recite it at the funeral.

FAIRY TREE
The building of a motorway in County Clare, Ireland, was rerouted and delayed for 10 years because of a fairy tree. According to legend, the hawthorn tree is a meeting point for the fairies of Munster when they go into battle with the fairies of Connacht, and so the local council was obliged to keep the new road from Limerick to Galway at least 16 ft (5 m) from the tree and erect a protective fence around it.

BONE WALLS
While working at St. Bavo's Cathedral in Ghent, Belgium, archaeologists discovered walls constructed out of human bones and shattered skulls. The majority of the walls are made of thigh and shin bones, with the spaces between filled with skulls. The walls are thought to have been built in the seventeenth or early eighteenth centuries using the bones of people who died in the second half of the fifteenth century.

TREE MAIL
The city of Melbourne, Australia, gave all of its 77,000 trees ID numbers and email addresses so that people could report on their health and general condition. Some residents started writing love letters to the trees or asking them difficult questions.

BUS RESTAURANT
In the Auvergne region of France, customers can enjoy gourmet cuisine on a double-decker bus. Chefs Charles and Mélina Moncouyoux run Le Bus 26, a restaurant in a bus that seats 26 people and drives off to a new location in the area every month.

The number of jars of Nutella sold in a year would be enough to cover the Great Wall of China eight times.

IRON RAIN
Wasp-76b, an exoplanet about 390 light-years away, has a temperature of 4,350°F (2,400°C) on its sunny side and is so hot that iron vaporizes in its atmosphere and falls on the cooler side of the planet as iron rain. Wasp-76b is nearly twice the size of Jupiter.

RAINBOW CHOCOLATE
By imprinting a special structure on the surface of the confectionery, scientists in Switzerland have created chocolate that has an ordinary dark-brown color under normal conditions but shimmers with rainbow colors when placed in direct light.

CAPTASTIC!
Venezuelan artist Oscar Olivares crafted an eco-mural from 200,000 recycled bottle caps and lids. The young artist collaborated with OkoSpiri and Movement in Architecture for the Future to collect the colorful caps from local citizens. The massive mural runs 141 ft (43 m) along the Plaza Escalona in El Hatillo Municipality, Caracas. It serves as a reminder to reduce, reuse, and recycle, when possible, as well as a celebration of hope for the future of the country.

IDENTITY CRISIS

The quirky appearance of the aptly named turtle frog (*Myobatrachus gouldii*) might just leave you scratching your head. Found in the sandy soils of Perth, Western Australia, this swollen pink creature has an oddly distinct, turtle-shaped head and loves to munch on termites. Its gold-flecked complexion, beady black eyes, and strange mouth give it the appearance of a turtle that's forgotten its shell. Stranger still, the turtle frog skips the tadpole stage altogether, transitioning from an egg straight to a tiny baby frog!

BIG BOB

Sengamalam, an elephant from Tamil Nadu, India, has gained fame worldwide for her bob-cut hairstyle. Her unique hairdo gets washed three times per day during the summer and at least once a day during other seasons. Her *mahout*, or caretaker, Mr. Rajagopal notes that the pachyderm's haircut is only possible because of her quiet, gentle nature and willingness to receive regular grooming.

VALENTINE'S CALF

A calf born at James McAuley's farm in County Antrim, Northern Ireland, on Valentine's Day 2020 had a perfectly shaped heart pattern on her forehead—and was named Be My Valentine.

SECOND BEST

If they are swimming near each other, alligators give manatees the right of way. Manatees wanting to pass through simply swim up to any alligators blocking their path and gently bump them out of the way.

LION STUDENT

An adult male lion was rescued from inside an elementary school in the Gir Somnath district of Gujarat, India. The lion had gone into a village in search of food but fled into the school after being disturbed and made his way up the stairs to the second floor. Fortunately, the school was empty at the time.

MILLION-DOLLAR PIGEON

Armando, a champion Belgian racing pigeon owned by Joël Verschoot, sold for more than $1.4 million USD at auction in 2019.

SWIMMING BAT

If knocked into the water, the greater bulldog bat from South America can swim by using its wings as oars. It is one of the few species of bat that has adapted to catch fish. It uses echolocation to detect water ripples made by fish and then extends its sharp claws to catch and cling on to its prey.

BARELY THERE

Not only do baby moray eels look nothing like their parents, they hardly look like anything at all due to their translucent serpentine appearance.

Baby morays pull off this neat feat by having no red blood cells, no bones, no spine, and only a thin muscle tissue layer. A gelatinous matrix supports their body, inviting comparisons to the aliens from *The Abyss* (1989). Their heads remain disproportionately tiny compared to the rest of their body. Their internal organs are also small, relying on a simple gut tube to digest nutrients. This lack of internal structure contributes to their near invisibility. As they grow into adults, their skin thickens, turning opaque. Their body length and depth changes, and they form red blood cells.

Adult moray eel.

LUSH LAYOVER

A destination in itself, the Changi Airport in Singapore has its own nature trails, butterfly and cactus gardens, and a fish spa!

The main attraction is the Jewel, a domed building at the center of which is a 130-ft-tall (40-m) cylindrical waterfall composed of harvested rainwater. Near the ceiling is a massive net where guests can balance their way above the indoor rainforest. Other entertainment includes a hedge maze, fog "bowls," sculptural playground slides, colorful topiaries, and high-tech interactive games. This is one airport where having a delayed flight is welcomed!

Holiday travelers enjoying artificial snow.

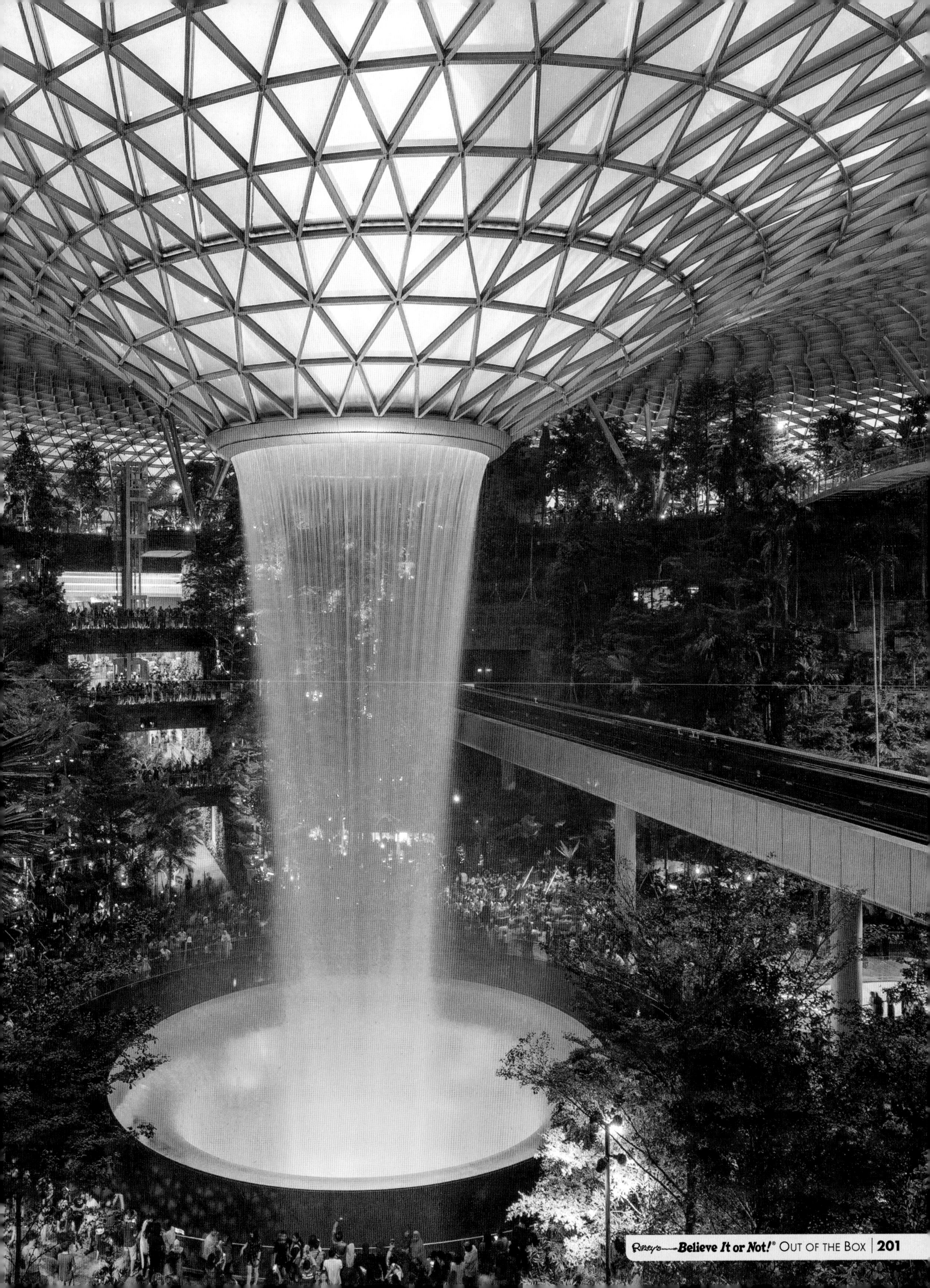

SLOW JOURNEY

The Nilgiri Mountain Railway, which transports passengers from Mettupalayam to Ooty in southern India, has an average speed of only 7 mph (11 kmph). It covers a distance of just 28.6 mi (46 km), but the uphill journey takes about 4 hours 50 minutes and the downhill journey around 3 hours 35 minutes.

BOTTLE BUILDING

A school in San Pablo, the Philippines, was built entirely out of recycled plastic soda bottles filled with adobe, a concrete substitute made of dirt, straw, and water.

PUMICE ISLAND

A floating 58-sq-mi (150-sq-km) pumice island, at least 6 in (15 cm) thick, was seen drifting in the ocean off Australia in 2019. The raft, which was more than twice the size of Manhattan, is thought to have been produced by an underwater volcanic explosion near Tonga. Pumice stone is buoyant because it is a highly porous, lightweight rock.

AIRPORT COURSE

An 18-hole golf course is laid out between the two runways at Don Mueang International Airport in Bangkok—Thailand's second busiest airport. There are no barriers to separate the course from either runway, and golfers rely on a red light to tell them when a plane is approaching.

EDIBLE PLATINUM

Chef Lazarius Ken Leysath Walker of The Twist restaurant in Columbia, South Carolina, created a $310 crab cake that features black truffles and is encrusted with edible platinum.

APOLOGY ACT

Canadians are renowned for being polite and for apologizing, so to protect them legally, the "Apology Act" was introduced in 2009 as a law in Ontario. It states that apologizing for an action does not imply an admission of fault or liability.

DOLL HEADS

The 1.5-mi-long (2.4-km) Doll's Head Trail in Constitution Lakes Park outside Atlanta, Georgia, is a hiking trail lined with creepy doll heads, like a scene from a horror movie. It was created by local carpenter Joel Slaton, who used trash he found on hikes through the park to build art displays incorporating dozens of dismembered doll heads.

COFFEE PHARAOH

The Grand Egyptian Museum in Giza created a mosaic portrait of the death mask of Pharaoh Tutankhamun, a.k.a. King Tut, with 7,260 cups of coffee! By combining more than 140 lb (65 kg) of coffee and 265 gal (1,000 l) of milk, organizers were able to achieve a variety of shades in order to recreate the boy king's likeness. The project took 12 hours to complete and covered an area of 646 sq ft (60 sq m).

TIP TOP TEMPLES

A narrow bridge over a heart-pounding gap in the summit connects the two temples.

Two Buddhist temples sit atop the Red Clouds Golden Summit, a 330-ft-tall (100-m) peak jutting from Mount Fanjing in the Wuling Mountains of southwestern China.

Buddhists have considered the site a holy place for centuries, with nearly 50 temples built on the mountainside since the Ming Dynasty more than 500 years ago. Many have since been destroyed, but the Temple of the Buddha and the Temple of Maitreya at the very top of the mountain were rebuilt according to their original appearance, plus extra reinforcement against strong winds. To reach these sacred buildings, you must climb 8,888 steps!

Many Buddhists believe that Mount Fanjing is a place where one can reach enlightenment.

FAKE FUNERALS

As a way to help curb rising suicide rates, programs in South Korea have started offering "living funerals" as a way for people to reflect on their lives. Most experiences include dressing in traditional burial clothing; writing eulogies, mock wills, and farewell notes; and lying in a coffin in a darkened room while meditating on life. Many participants have left the program with a greater appreciation of their lives.

COUCH CASH

Howard Kirby found $43,000 stashed inside the cushion of a couch he had bought for $35 from a thrift store in Owosso, Michigan. Howard thought the cushion felt hard, unzipped it, and he found the cash inside. He generously returned the money to the couch's surprised former owners.

BLUE BLOOD

The blood of a 25-year-old woman from Providence, Rhode Island, turned dark blue after she took medication containing benzocaine to numb a toothache. It triggered a rare reaction that led to a condition called *methemoglobinemia*, which can cause blue blood and skin.

FIRST NEWS

Johnny Cash claimed to be the first American to know about the death of Soviet leader Joseph Stalin in 1953! Cash's job as a radio operator in the U.S. military was to intercept Soviet messages, one of which reported Stalin's death. If his claim is true, he may have known about it before President Eisenhower!

AGED TO PRESERVATION

A family in Michigan has a 143-year-old fruitcake that has been passed down through five generations! Fidelia Ford made the dessert in 1878 and intended to serve it after a year of aging. Sadly, Fidelia died before the year passed, and her husband couldn't bring himself to cut the cake. Instead, it has been passed down through the family and is now in possession of Julie Ruttinger—Fidelia's great-great-granddaughter. In 2003, the fruitcake made an appearance on the *Tonight Show*, where Jay Leno tasted a small piece of the rock-hard dessert!

MOTHER 1878. November 28

LASTING LEGACY

The body of Russian revolutionary leader Vladimir Lenin has been kept on display since he died in 1924.

The body currently resides in "Lenin's Mausoleum" in Moscow's Red Square. It costs Russia about $200,000 a year to preserve his body and keep it looking as lifelike as possible. A team of about six people dubbed the "Mausoleum group" are responsible for maintaining the deceased politician's appearance. Every 18 months, the body takes a month-and-a-half-long bath in various embalming fluids.

Unlike mummification, which changes the appearance and texture of a body in order to preserve the original parts, the goal of embalming is to keep the body looking and feeling as it did in life, even if that means the body isn't 100 percent original. Lenin's internal organs were removed and damaged tissue gets replaced with plastic, wax, or other materials.

No photography is allowed inside Lenin's Mausoleum, making photos of his body rare.

Dr. Emslie found this even older, 1,000-year-old penguin mummy at a nearby site, Cape Barne.

DEFROSTED FOWL

During a research trip to Cape Irizar, Ross Sea, Antarctica, in 2016, ornithologist Dr. Steven Emslie discovered the mummified remains of 800-year-old penguins!

The finding bewildered Emslie at first, because the carcasses appeared fresh, yet there was no record of penguins living in that area for the past 100 years. It turns out the remains had been buried under snow and ice for hundreds of years, preserving everything from bones and feathers to droppings and eggshells. Warming caused by climate change melted the ice to reveal these ancient Adélie penguin colonies.

HAIR GLASSES

Tom Broughton's British company Cubitts makes eyeglass frames out of various waste products, including potatoes, old CDs, yogurt cups, and human hair.

FAKE BILL

In 2019, a man unsuccessfully tried to open a bank account in Lincoln, Nebraska, with a fake $1 million bill. The largest denomination note ever issued for public circulation in the United States was the $10,000 bill.

FIRST BABIES

Katrin Guðjónsdóttir, the first baby born in Iceland in 1980, went on to give birth to the first baby born in Iceland in 2017.

GIGANTIC PUZZLE

Kodak launched a gigantic 51,300-piece jigsaw puzzle measuring 28.5 × 6.25 ft (8.7 × 1.9 m). It features images of 27 international landmarks, including the Statue of Liberty and the Taj Mahal, all shot by professional photographers.

STILL WORKING

Erica Bennett lost her iPhone when it fell overboard from a boat into the Edisto River in South Carolina—but a diver found it 15 months later, and it still worked.

FREE FISH

From 1884 to 1894, residents of Baltimore, Maryland, or Washington, D.C., could write to their congressman and receive a free goldfish. Around 20,000 were given away each year before the program was halted.

HOT HEADED

At the 1936 Municipal Exhibition in Berlin, Germany, "fireproof suits" designed for air raids made their debut. Similar to deep-sea diving equipment, they enclosed wearers from head to toe. The top of each helmet featured a sprinkler, fueled by a connection to a hose and ejecting a powerful spray of water. A simple hand lever allowed one to control the spray's pressure. Despite the "innovative" suit, it never saw wide use, as the design contributed to nasty steam burns.

TWIN BIRTHS

Alexzandria Wolliston of West Palm Beach, Florida, gave birth to two sets of twins in 2019. Mark and Malakhi were born on March 13, followed by Kaylen and Kaleb just over nine months later on December 27.

UNIQUE ORGANS

The lungs are the only organs of the human body that can float on water.

FIRST BABY

When Luciana Golato was born to parents Joe and Jeanne on January 27, 2020, she was the first baby to be born in Sea Isle City, New Jersey, in more than 40 years.

BULLET REMOVED

A man in Connecticut who found it painful to urinate had a bullet removed from his bladder 18 years after being shot.

SNOW CONE

During the winter months, British Columbia's Helmcken Falls transform into a one-of-a-kind snow waterfall and crater you've got to see to believe. When temperatures drop below freezing, it creates the perfect conditions for the falls' free-flowing water to transform into snowflakes midair. As this new snow accumulates at the bottom, it creates a unique "snow cone." The fourth-largest waterfall in Canada, Helmcken features a 463-ft (141-m) drop. This unique snow feature sits against the dramatic backdrop of Wells Gray Provincial Park, located north of Kamloops.

1 You Gandhi Be Kidding

Mahatma Gandhi's dedication to peaceful protest has inspired generations to take the high road. So have quotes like "Be the change you'd like to see in the world." Unfortunately, Gandhi never made this wise statement, although it accurately sums up his philosophy.

...OR NOT! QUOTE EDITION

Sometimes a misconception gets repeated so often that many end up believing it's a fact.

Here at Ripley's, we like to call that an "Or Not!" because you can't always "Believe It!" Check this list of Or Not! facts before posting that inspirational quote on Instagram.

2 Girl Power

While Marilyn Monroe's life proved emblematic of the quotation "Well-behaved women rarely make history," she never made this claim. Instead, Laurel Thatcher Ulrich, a writer and Harvard professor, coined it in 1976.

3 One Small Misquote

Neil Armstrong's "That's one small step for man, one giant leap for mankind" remains iconic. But Armstrong maintained for years that he'd said "a man" rather than "man." A 2006 computer analysis confirmed the astronaut's story, identifying the missing word.

5 Bready or Not

When commoners starved in Paris, Marie Antoinette counseled, "Let them eat cake." Her blatant disregard for suffering was rewarded with beheading by the mob. Yet history notes she actually said "brioche," a cross between pastry and bread, instead of cake.

4 Wilde-ly Misquoted

No one said it better than Oscar Wilde, "Be yourself; everyone else is already taken." Except Wilde's original quote proved far less pithy: "Most people are other people. Their thoughts are someone else's opinions, their lives a mimicry, their passions a quotation."

SCALED FASHION

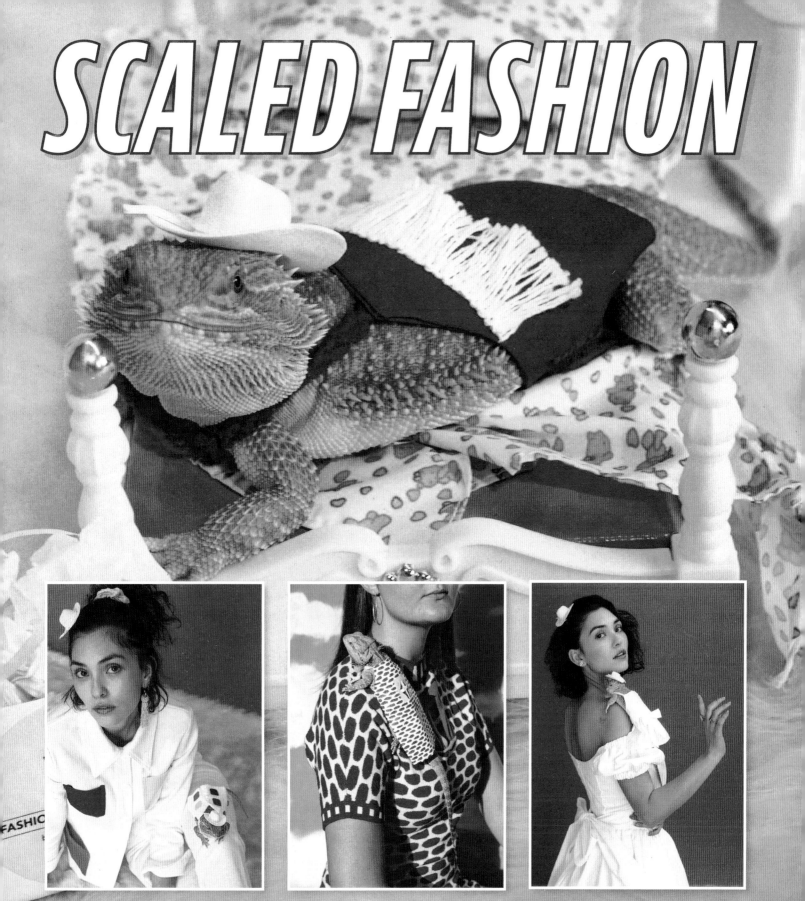

For the reptile enthusiast who has everything, this year's hottest gifts are matching human and lizard outfits created by Los Angeles fashion designer Penelope Gazin.

Gazin has made more than 20 different articles of clothing for lizards, which are sold under her Fashion Brand Company label. Her reasoning behind the unique line of clothing? "I hate lizards," she says, "So I wanted to create clothes to cover up their disgusting bodies." From matching red-and-white patterned dresses to loud sweaters that would turn any lounge lizard's head, reptiles and their human owners have plenty of fashionable "twinning" options.

missing eye but to help them see in the dark. It takes the average human eye about 25 minutes to adjust from bright sunlight to being able to see in total darkness, so when going below deck, pirates would swap the patch from one eye to the other in order to see with the eye that had already adjusted to darkness.

EXPLODING HEAD

Jill Lafferty, of Woodbury, New Jersey, has been diagnosed with a rare condition called exploding head syndrome, which causes her to imagine loud banging sounds while she is asleep. The sleep disorder has caused her to hear imaginary gunshots outside her home that were so realistic she called the police.

FAKE FLAMINGOS

There are more fake plastic flamingos in the world than real ones. There are an estimated 250,000 real flamingos compared to millions of lawn ornaments.

SPACE VOTE

Drew Morgan, an astronaut on the International Space Station, voted in a 2019 Pennsylvania election via an absentee ballot from space.

JESUS SAVED

During the 2019 Twin Cities 10-Mile race in Minneapolis, Minnesota, Tyler Moon, a runner wearing "Jesus Saves" on his racing bib, suffered a heart attack—and one of the people who helped revive him was another competitor, named Jesus Bueno!

BRIDGE PROPOSAL

Dan Del Tufo and fellow civil engineer Julia Kallmerten took their engagement to new heights on the vertical-lift Memorial Bridge in Portsmouth, New Hampshire, raised to its maximum height. Both had worked on projects near the bridge. Traffic was temporarily blocked when Del Tufo went down on one knee the moment the bridge was raised to its highest point.

INDESTRUCTIBLE JACKET

Dutch adventure clothing brand Vollebak sells a puffer jacket with an exterior made of Dyneema, a fiber that is 15 times stronger than steel. Although the material is lightweight, it is so strong that during testing, it stopped rounds from a Kalashnikov assault rifle.

EYE WORM

Doctors removed a 2.8-in-long (7-cm), wriggling parasitic worm from the eyeball of 70-year-old Jasubhai Patel, of Gujarat, India. They think the worm entered his eye when he was bitten by a dog 12 years earlier.

PAINTING WITH LIGHT

LumiLor is an electroluminescent paint that illuminates when you pass electricity through it.

Unlike glow-in-the-dark paint, which loses its nighttime brilliance quickly, LumiLor lights up when, where, and how you choose. Designed by the aftermarket painter Andy Zsinko, it relies on a base coat that conducts an electric current. Professional painters can apply it to various surfaces, from plastic to metal, wood to fiberglass, and even carbon fiber, resulting in illuminated helmets, motorcycles, electric guitars, and more.

1200

MEGA PERFORMANCE

CLIFFHANGER

Situated off the coast of Iceland's Vestmannaeyjar (Westman Islands), Þridrangaviti Lighthouse offers extreme coastal living. Perched precariously atop a rocky pillar jutting up from the Atlantic Ocean, the lighthouse lies on an island about 6 mi (9.6 km) from shore. It is accessible by helicopter today, which beats how construction workers reached the site in 1938 during the building process. Before copters, the workers ascended the 120-foot-high (36.5-m) rock, laying the foundation by hand.

PALATIAL SCHOOL

Russian businessman Andrei Simanovsky is transforming his old 1940s-built school in Yekaterinburg into an extravagant French Baroque palace, complete with golden chandeliers, gilded walls, marble floors, and a water fountain. The 106 Secondary School has seen a sudden surge in student numbers since the incredible makeover started.

AGED COFFEE

The Münch, a coffeehouse in Osaka, Japan, serves 22-year-old coffee for $900 a cup. The owner, Kanji Tanaka, had the idea for aging coffee after he found that a batch of ice coffee which he accidentally left in the fridge for six months had acquired a unique flavor.

RUNWAY CROSSING

The Napier to Gisborne railway line in New Zealand crosses the main runway of Gisborne Airport. Trains have to stop and get clearance from the air traffic control tower before proceeding.

RED BEACH

Every year, an entire beach in Panjin, China, glows bright red. Red Beach is covered in a type of seaweed called *Suaeda salsa* that glows a fiery red color in the fall.

COAL RIDE

The world's first roller coaster was built to transport coal down a hill. The Mauch Chunk and Summit Railroad in eastern Pennsylvania opened in 1827 to carry coal that miners had dug out of the nearby mountains, descending 936 ft (285 m) along its 9-mi (14.4-km) journey. It reached a speed of 50 mph (80 kmph) on its descent, prompting visitors to ask if they, too, could ride in the open carts for a few cents. Among those who rode on the railroad was LaMarcus Adna Thompson, who saw its potential for entertainment and went on to build the Switchback Railway at Coney Island, America's first official roller coaster.

SNOWBALL FIGHT

The University of British Columbia in Vancouver, Canada, postponed its annual snowball fight on January 15, 2020, because there was too much snow.

DEEP MINE

The Mponeng gold mine in South Africa extends more than 2.5 mi (4 km) below ground and is so deep that 10 Empire State Buildings could fit inside atop each other. The journey from the surface to the bottom of the mine takes over an hour.

MAIN ISLANDS

There are 6,852 islands in Japan, but just four of them—Hokkaido, Honshu, Kyushu, and Shikoku—make up 97 percent of the country's total land area.

BIG AND TALL

From the running of the bulls to La Tomatina, Spanish festivals feature colorful parades where *cabezudos* (bigheads) and *gigantes* (giants) roam the streets!

The person wearing the cabezudo looks out through the mouth and wears a harness to help control the movements. Balance is vital, as their role is to chase and hit parade-goers with foam sacks! The cabezudos are almost always accompanied by gigantes, or giants, that stand 9 to 13 ft tall (3 to 4 m). They usually come in female and male pairs, modeled after characters from local folklore. At crowded festivals where things go by in a blur, sometimes bigger is better!

PINE AND DINE

Considered the "most festive pub in London," the Churchill Arms decorates 86 pine trees planted along its exterior façade with 22,500 lights each Christmas season. The pub holds an official lighting ceremony to ring in the season the first week of December. The event includes mulled wine, mincemeat pies, and Christmas carols.

GRADUATE CROSSING

After COVID-19 led to school and university closures, the class of 2020 took matters into their own hands, hosting graduation ceremonies in *Animal Crossing: New Horizons*. The game's custom clothing tools allowed students to create graduation caps and gowns. They set up virtual stages with podiums and handed out digital diplomas. XQ America got in on the action with its Graduate Together Project. The Project included a live-streamed event on May 16, 2020, providing a nationwide platform for graduates.

JELL-O HORSE

In the movie *The Wizard of Oz*, "the horse of a different color" was created by covering a white horse in colored Jell-O paste. Those scenes had to be shot quickly because the horse kept trying to lick it off.

STRAY CAT

The gray and white cat held by Marlon Brando in the opening scene of *The Godfather* was a stray found on the Paramount lot by director Francis Ford Coppola. The cat was so content that its loud purring muffled some of Brando's dialogue, which later had to be edited and looped.

POPULAR VOTE

Americans cast more votes for Taylor Hicks to win season five of the TV show *American Idol* than they did for Ronald Reagan in the 1984 presidential election.

TIMELY AUDITION

When Matt LeBlanc auditioned for *Friends*, he had only $11 to his name. With his first paycheck he bought a hot meal.

TRACED HEADSTONE

As a child, *Frankenstein* author Mary Shelley learned to write by tracing the letters on her mother Mary Wollstonecraft's headstone.

NOISY NEIGHBORS

Much of the Eagles' album *Hotel California* was recorded at Criteria Studios in Miami, Florida, where UK heavy metal band Black Sabbath was in the next studio. Sabbath was so loud that the Eagles' closing ballad "The Last Resort" had to be re-recorded multiple times due to noise leakage through the studio wall.

ALBUM IMAGE

At first, actress Mae West refused to grant permission to the Beatles to use her image on the cover of their album *Sgt. Pepper's Lonely Hearts Club Band*, but she changed her mind after they each sent her a personal letter.

FAN FEED

UNBELIEVABLE TRIBUTE

Artist Nicoletta Bates of Southampton, Pennsylvania, painted an homage to Ripley's Believe It or Not! on a jean jacket. Using acrylic paints, Bates recreated the likeness of Liu Ch'ung, a man with two pupils in each eye who appeared in some of the earliest Ripley's Believe It or Not! cartoons and books. Featured prominently in the middle is the stylized "R" from our logo. And the Japanese characters on the side? They translate to "believe it or not," of course!

BRICK BY BRICK

Sean Kenney's award-winning art exhibition *Nature Connects* contains whimsical statues crafted from millions of LEGO bricks.

For the past decade, Kenney has transformed LEGO into masterpieces. Working in vibrant plastic bricks, his finished sculptures present pixelated portrayals of daily life. Along with a Brooklyn-based team of artists, Kenney spends years creating the pieces for each exhibition. His sculptures reflect complex themes like natural harmony and humanity's relationship with nature. Subjects include enormous bees, butterflies, flowers, and even human beings.

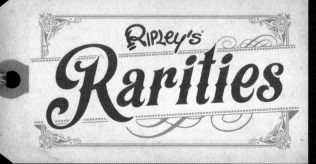
Ripley's Exhibit
Cat. No. 173669

BATHYSPHERE

Replica of an unpowered
submersible from the early
1930s. This invention could hold
two people and revolutionized
deep-sea exploration. Attached
to a cable, the Bathysphere
could reach depths of more than
3,000 ft (914 m)!

Ripley's Exhibit
Cat. No. 9233

ROBERT RIPLEY'S SUITCASE

The founder of Ripley's Believe It or Not!, Robert Ripley,
visited 201 countries over his lifetime. Decals from his
travels can be seen on his suitcase here, including the
1933 Chicago World's Fair, where the first Odditorium
was showcased.

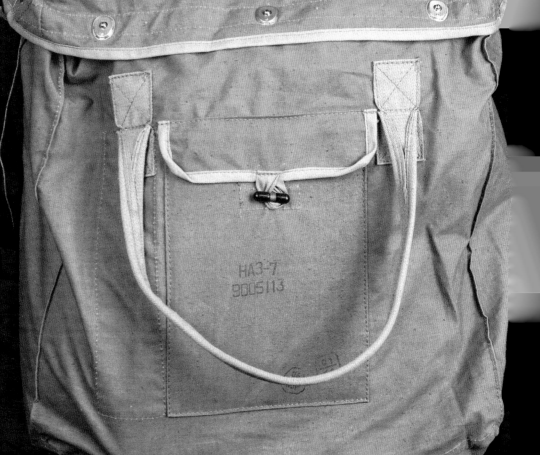

Ripley's Exhibit
Cat. No. 173635

COSMONAUT SURVIVAL KIT

Late 1980s satchel designed for cosmonauts (the Soviet Union's term for astronauts) in emergency landing situations. Items in this pack include a looped razor-wire saw, a compass, fishing equipment, folding metal skis, a medical kit, boxes for flares and bullets, a flashlight, matches, a signal mirror, water purification supplies, a plastic box for food, and more!

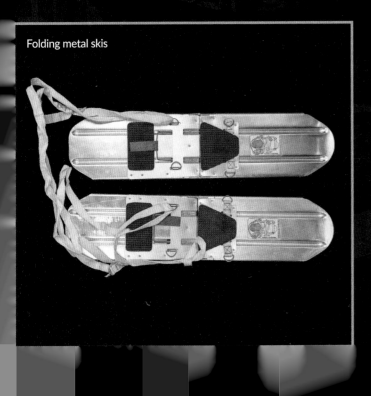

Folding metal skis

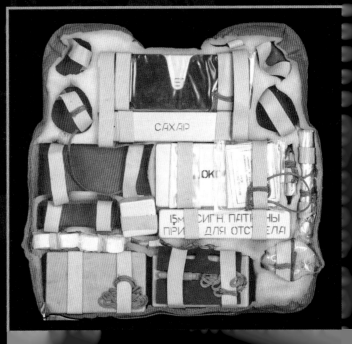

MIGHTY BITE

The titan beetle of South America grows up to 6.5 in (16.5 cm) long and has such powerful jaws that its bite can snap a pencil in two.

HARD STARE

Researchers at England's University of Exeter claim that you can stop a seagull from stealing your food just by staring at the bird.

GENTLE TOUCH

On several occasions, Jennifer Ahlberg's Labrador-Pyrenees mix, Gus, helped birds trapped inside their home's enclosed porch by gently catching them in his mouth and then releasing them outside.

GIANT SNAIL

The giant triton snail can grow up to 18 in (45 cm) long and is able to kill and eat starfish by paralyzing them with its venomous saliva.

BEE BITE

When pollen sources are scarce, bumblebees deliberately bite the leaves of certain plants to make them flower up to a month early.

PENGUIN HUDDLE

To keep out the bitterly cold Antarctic winds, emperor penguins form mass huddles consisting of hundreds of birds. They even rotate their positions with the birds at the center of the huddle (where heat is most easily retained), moving to the outside to ensure that every penguin stays as warm as possible.

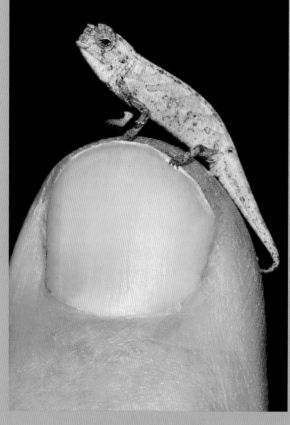

LITTLE LIZARD

Discovered on the island of Madagascar, the *Brookesia nana* chameleon is likely the smallest reptile in the world! The females max out at about 1.1 in (29 mm), but the males are even smaller at just 0.9 in (22 mm) long—and that's including the tail! A phenomenon known as the "island effect" has resulted in many miniature species evolving on Madagascar, such as the pygmy mouse lemur, but researchers are unsure if that's why the nano-chameleon is so small.

EEL SHOCK

A newly discovered electric eel from the Amazon, *Electrophorus voltai*, can discharge 860 volts of electricity—more than seven times the voltage of a standard light bulb.

SNAKES SURPRISE

More than 150 garter snakes were removed from beneath the back deck of Shaynon McFadden and Royce Robins's home in Elizabeth, Colorado.

SHEEP BRA

After Rose the sheep suffered damage to her udders on a farm near Auckland, New Zealand, veterinarian Dr. Sarah Clews fitted her with a human maternity bra for three weeks until they healed.

CAR CRUSHER

The bite of a *Tyrannosaurus rex* exerted around six to seven tons of pressure that would have been powerful enough to crush a car.

DRUG DESTROYERS

Wild boars in Tuscany, Italy, sniffed out and destroyed more than $20,000 worth of drugs that had been buried in a forest by dealers.

REPORTED MISSING

When Chico the German shepherd mix got lost, he walked into his local police station in Odessa, Texas, in the middle of the night, put his paws on the counter, and reported himself missing! He lived about 1 mi (1.6 km) from the station and was soon reunited with owner Edward Alvarado.

IRON SNAIL

The scaly-foot snail grows its own armor! Not only is its shell covered with iron, but it also grows chainmail-like metal plates on its fleshy "foot." Researchers think these adaptations might provide protection from predators, such as crabs. To top it all off, this hardcore gastropod lives alongside deep-sea hydrothermal vents in the Indian Ocean, where the water can reach up to 750°F (400°C)!

SKIN DEEP

When Surinam toadlets are ready to be born, they literally burst out of their mother's skin!

How did they get there to begin with, you ask? Well, after the eggs are fertilized, the male pushes them onto the female's back. They stick there for a couple of days while the mother's skin begins to grow over them. The eggs then hatch, develop for a few months, and once fully formed—POP! Out into the world they go, leaving their mother covered with tiny craters.

GREENERY SCENERY

About 2,000 fishermen moved from Houtouwan village on Shengshan Island in the early 1990s, leaving their once-thriving town to the ravages of time and vegetation overgrowth.

Life in this remote Chinese village, which resides on one of more than 400 islands in the Shengsi archipelago, comes with few amenities, as the handful of remaining residents can attest. Yet, as plants continue to cover the city's decrepit houses, it has inspired renewed activity in the form of tourism. Visitors now flock to the area to photograph its plant-submerged structures, a testament to nature's most picturesque reclamation project.

0.75 IN
(2 CM)
ACTUAL SIZE!

SMALL START

Called a joey, a newborn koala weighs just 0.02 oz (0.5 g) and is the size of a jelly bean!

Even though it is born blind and without ears or fur, it can immediately climb unaided into the safety of its mother's pouch, where it stays for about seven months. During the last month or so in the pouch, the joey will poke its head out to eat a specialized type of feces called "pap" from the mother's butt! Pap is mushy, protein-rich, and necessary for preparing the baby koala's digestive system for eucalyptus leaves.

SCIENCE SLOTH

SlothBot, a slow-moving, solar-powered robot, travels along a cable between trees to collect data affecting endangered species.

It was built by a team of robotics engineers from the Georgia Institute of Technology, who sought design inspiration from actual sloths. It monitors weather, carbon dioxide levels, temperatures, and other information only observable through continuous presence over many months or even years. Researchers see it as an exciting new development in the application of robotics for conservation.

ONLINE SHOP

When zookeeper Lv Mengmeng left her cellphone in a room at Yancheng Wild Animal World in Jiangsu Province, China, a quick-thinking baboon used it to make several online purchases. Mengmeng was surprised to find messages confirming orders to her shopping cart and when she checked the surveillance footage, she saw the baboon pick up her phone with its hands and swipe left and right on the screen.

FIRE ESCAPE

Danielle Schafer was asleep in bed when a fire raged through her Lansing, New York, apartment block—until her rescue cat Kitty jumped on her. Thanks to her pet's vigilance, Schafer got out safely, and although Kitty was unable to escape from the bedroom at the time, she survived the deadly, black smoke by burying herself in Schafer's pillows for the next seven hours before a firefighter rescued her the following morning from the smoldering rubble of the block.

WASHER ORDEAL

Posey the kitten survived 20 minutes inside a washing machine after owner Courtney Drury, from Liverpool, England, put in the clothes and switched on the cycle, unaware that the little cat had jumped in. When Drury heard meowing from inside, she forced open the door and gave a wet Posey CPR to save her life.

ROWDY ROOSTER

A retired couple on the small island of Oléron, located off France's Atlantic coast, unsuccessfully sued for a noise complaint against their neighbor Corinne Fesseau's rooster Maurice, whose daily dawn crowing annoyed them.

FREAK OUTAGE

A walleye fish that was dropped from the sky by a bird landed on a pole-mounted transformer and caused a power outage to homes in North Bay, Ontario, Canada, on September 19, 2019.

CURIOUS CUBS

Two bear cubs were rescued after they locked themselves inside a van and then honked the horn repeatedly for help. Security technician Jeff Stokely had parked his van outside a customer's house in Gatlinburg, Tennessee, but the cubs climbed in through the driver-side door and accidentally shut themselves in. When Stokely heard the horn, he went to investigate and set the bears free.

PET PORTRAIT

Kathy Smith, from Corwen, Wales, spent an entire week creating a family photo of her 17 dogs and cats. It took her seven days to get her eight dogs and nine cats lined up, sitting on and around the sofa, and all looking at the camera at the same time.

GRANNY CARE

Young orcas are much more likely to survive if they have a living grandmother in the group to look after them and help them find salmon feeding grounds.

CURIOUS CROW CONDUCT

Crows are some of the smartest birds around—they can remember faces, use gestures to communicate, and use tools, among other things. Their high intelligence means that sometimes their behavior can get a little bit... unusual.

CRANKY CROW

George the crow vandalized the windshield wipers of more than 20 cars in Essex, England, over a two-month period, forcing drivers to protect them with tarps and blankets. No one is sure what caused his behavior. But even two fake owls and a hawk-shaped kite that were installed in an attempt to stop his attacks have not prevented him from going after the wipers.

SEEKING REVENGE

Shiva Kewat, a laborer from Madhya Pradesh, India, has been constantly attacked by crows for more than three years after he was accidentally involved in the death of a young crow. He is attacked whenever he leaves home and says the birds specifically target him and nobody else, forcing him to fend them off with a stick.

SNACK TIME

Crows in Japanese cities have been seen dropping a walnut on a pedestrian crossing, waiting for a car to crack open the nut by driving over it, and then swooping to eat the cracked nut in safety as soon as the pedestrian light turns green.

16 FT (5 M) OF HAIR!

ON LOCKDOWN

Nguyen Van Chien from Vietnam hasn't cut his hair in more than 80 years! He also hasn't combed or washed it in that time, either. The result is giant, 16-ft-long (5-m) mass of hair that his son helps manage. Chien stopped cutting his hair after the third grade, in response to what he considered a divine calling. Today, he keeps it all safely coiled on his head under a scarf.

COCKROACH FAMILY
A 24-year-old man went to a hospital in China's Guangdong Province, complaining of sharp pain in his right ear. When doctors examined him, they discovered a family of 11 cockroaches—a full-grown adult and 10 of its offspring—running around in his ear canal.

COINCIDENTAL NAME
A meteorite had not fallen to Earth in the region of Paris, France, for more than 400 years until 2011, when one crashed into the home of a family named... Comette. The egg-shaped rock, believed to be 4.57 billion years old, smashed through the roof of Martine Comette's home while the family was away on vacation.

URINE TROUBLE
Two Chinese doctors, Zhang Hong and Xiao Zhangxiang, saved an elderly man with a badly swollen stomach on a flight from Guangzhou, China, to New York City by sucking the urine out of his bladder for 40 minutes. They constructed a makeshift device using tubing from one of the plane's oxygen masks, and Dr. Zhang managed to suck out 1.8 pints (1 liter) of urine that was trapped in the man's bladder. Dr. Zhang spat the urine into an empty wine bottle.

TOILET AIDE
Sir Henry Norris, who was executed in 1536 for committing adultery with English king Henry VIII's wife Anne Boleyn, was a Groom of the Stool, responsible for assisting the king with going to the toilet.

RECORDED DELIVERY
Police officer Jeremy Dean was patrolling busy rush-hour traffic in West Valley City, Utah, on February 11, 2020, when a driver flagged him down to say that his wife was about to give birth inside their vehicle. Traffic came to a standstill while Dean donned gloves and helped the woman to deliver her baby—and the whole episode was recorded by Dean's body camera.

TEXT MESSAGES
It is estimated that the average person will text about 2 million words or more in a lifetime.

TASTY ALTERNATIVE
In 2019, students with unpaid parking fines at the University of Alaska's Anchorage campus were given the option of paying their fines with jars of peanut butter, jelly, or other sandwich spreads.

DRONE CAPTURE
Struggling to cope with the steep cliffs in Yunnan Province, Chinese police eventually used drones to track down fugitive Song Moujiang, who had been on the run for 17 years and was holed up in a tiny mountain cave.

RIBBIT EXHIBIT

In a small museum in the town of Estavayer-le-Lac, Switzerland, there are 108 stuffed frogs posed in scenes from everyday life in the mid-1800s.

The official name of the museum is Musée d'Estavayer-le-Lac et ses grenouilles, or "Museum of Estavayer-le-Lac and its frogs," but it is more commonly known as the Frog Museum. Legend has it that the taxidermied amphibians were created more than 150 years ago by an officer named François Perrier. The artist took great care in crafting the furniture and props for the miniature scenes, from the patterns on a miniscule deck of cards to a cigarette hanging precariously from a pool-playing frog's mouth.

COLLECTION ROYALE

Stephen Sherrard-Griffith of Melbourne, Australia, boasts a James Bond collection more than 21 years and $55,000 in the making! He has more than 4,000 pieces of memorabilia filling three rooms of his home. The one-time filmmaker has now made amassing Bond paraphernalia a full-time job. His collection boasts rare figurines, film posters, and books worth thousands of dollars.

POODLE PIECE
One of Ludwig van Beethoven's earliest musical compositions was an elegy for a dead poodle.

SPOCK CUT
When *Star Trek* first became a hit on TV in the 1960s, Leonard Nimoy's father Max worked as a barber in Boston, Massachusetts. Customers would go into his barbershop and ask for a "Spock cut," not knowing that Spock's father was cutting their hair!

DAILY WALK
U.S. actor Terry O'Quinn, who played John Locke in the TV series *Lost*, regularly walked 12 mi (19 km) a day to and from the set.

RARE TOY
A rare 1979 Boba Fett *Star Wars* action figure prototype sold at auction in 2019 for $157,500. The toy's scarcity is due to the fact that it never went on sale because of safety concerns, its rocket firing mechanism was thought to be too dangerous.

PEN PAL
Edgar Allan Poe liked to write with his Siamese cat perched on his shoulder. He would place the cat there before he started writing a poem to make him feel more relaxed and draw inspiration.

FIRE SERVICE
Star Wars creator George Lucas has his own fire truck and employs 14 full-time firefighters at his workplace, Skywalker Ranch, near Nicasio, California.

POP PATENTS

You're sure to recognize the names on this list, but you might be surprised to learn that in addition to being celebrities, they're also inventors! Check out the innovative patents these household names have filed.

BILL NYE
The Science Guy inspired generations of kids to get excited about the natural world, but he also has an interest in the arts—he invented a ballet slipper offering superior support to dancers!

JAMES CAMERON
The director of Hollywood blockbusters like *Titanic* and *Avatar* invented a self-propelled underwater dolly permitting divers to move effortlessly through the water while filming.

HARRY HOUDINI
A famed escape artist and magician, he also dabbled in inventions, creating a diving suit that the wearer could easily exit while submerged underwater.

JAMIE LEE CURTIS
From *True Lies* to *Freaky Friday*, this actress made the "mom" role iconic, and she's continued this work offscreen by designing a diaper with a waterproof baby wipe–holding compartment.

MICHAEL JACKSON
It's fitting that the creator of the *Moonwalk* invented gravity-defying boots with a moveable hitch, allowing the wearer to lean unnaturally forward, as seen in his iconic "Smooth Criminal" music video.

BURNING LOVE

Professional UK stuntman Ricky Ash proposed to his girlfriend, British nurse Katrina Dobson, while engulfed in flames!

Despite being an unlikely matchup—Ash is 5 ft 3 in (1.6 m) and Dobson is 6 ft 3 in (1.9 m)—passion ignited after the pair met online. Ash, who has appeared in blockbusters like Tim Burton's *Sleepy Hollow* (1999), credits his short stature as the key to his success. In 2000, he entered the record books as the world's most versatile stuntman. Yet the scorching proposal remains his most rewarding feat.

BALLET RIOT

When Russian composer Igor Stravinsky's ballet *The Rite of Spring* was first performed in Paris, France, in 1913, it was received so badly that audience members rioted and threw objects at the orchestra.

FREESTYLE RAP

Pittsburgh, Pennsylvania, rapper Frzy performed a freestyle rap for 31 hours straight in January 2020.

POTHOLE MOSAICS

Jim Bachor, an artist from Chicago, Illinois, repairs street potholes by cementing colorful ice cream mosaics over them.

HAT SPAT

Boston Red Sox fan Ben Affleck refused to wear a New York Yankees baseball cap for a scene in the movie *Gone Girl*. He and director David Fincher eventually agreed on a compromise where Affleck's character wore a Mets cap.

TOO SLOW

The song "Over the Rainbow" was deleted from *The Wizard of Oz* by producers after an early preview because they thought it "slowed down the picture." It was later reinstated and won an Academy Award for Best Original Song and became Judy Garland's signature number.

POTATO ASTEROID

The *Star Wars: The Empire Strikes Back* special effects department used several potatoes to look like distant asteroids during a chase sequence.

STORE NAME

Actress Halle Berry was named after Halle Brothers Co. Department store, a major landmark in her birthplace of Cleveland, Ohio.

MUMMY'S FOOT

As a souvenir from a trip to the Middle East, nineteenth-century French novelist Gustave Flaubert brought home a mummy's foot and kept it on his writing desk.

ON THE HUNT

Every October, the far western Mongolian province of Bayan-Ölgii hosts the Golden Eagle Festival, attracting spectators from all over the globe fascinated by the incredible exploits of Kazakh *burkitshi*, or eagle hunters.

The *burkitshi* tradition dates back to Kublai Khan's reign. A grandson and successor of Genghis Khan, Kublai Khan led massive hunts, employing thousands of falconers and golden eagles. Today, the Golden Eagle Festival keeps this tradition alive for all to see. In 2020, the event marked its twentieth anniversary with more than 120 competitors, ranging in age from 10 to 82 years old.

Although the festival pays homage to the ancient Mongolian-Kazakh hunting tradition, no hunting takes place. Instead, judges rank participants by their Kazakh costumes' intricacy, the elegance of their eagles in flight, horsemanship, and nuances in skill. The two-day festival culminates with an awards ceremony where winning falconers receive money, medals, and tiny medallions for their eagles. To compete, hunters raise birds from chicks, training them for ten years of service before releasing them back into the wild.

FLOATING FUNGUS

Katy Ayers of Kearney, Nebraska, grew a working, 8-ft-long (2.4-m) canoe out of mushrooms!

Known as "Myconoe," the boat is made from mycelium, the fibrous, dense roots of a mushroom that typically grow beneath the soil. Ayers built the watercraft from a wooden skeleton covered in mushroom spawn, with help from Ash Gordon of the Nebraska Mushroom farm. They suspended the structure in a room where the temperature ranged between 80 to 90°F (27 to 32°C) and the humidity was 90 to 100 percent. Then, nature took over. In September 2019, Ayers successfully rowed across Eagle Scout Lake in Grand Island to raise awareness about the many ways fungi can help clean up the environment, like slowing climate change and fighting pollution.

LOST PURSE

While demolishing part of the old Jeffersonville High School in Indiana in 2019, workers found a black purse behind science classroom cabinets belonging to Martha Ingham (now Martha Everett), a senior at the school in 1955. The purse, which contained a prom invitation, lipstick, photos, and Juicy Fruit gum wrappers, was returned to 82-year-old Everett at her home in Englewood, Florida.

LOTTO FRAUD

Two men were arrested in Flowood, Mississippi, on suspicion of trying to claim a $100,000 lotto jackpot by gluing the winning numbers onto a losing ticket.

SERIAL OFFENDER

Tommy Johns, of Brisbane, Australia, was arrested nearly 3,000 times for being drunk between 1957 and his death from a brain tumor in 1988.

SUPPORT BEER

Floyd Hayes, from Brooklyn, New York, loves beer so much that he registered a pint of it as an emotional support animal to carry on public transportation.

MAIL HOARD

A 61-year-old postal worker from Yokohama, Japan, was arrested for hoarding 24,000 items of mail that he had failed to deliver for 16 years, since 2003.

SURPLUS HENS

When Steve Morrow, of Hamilton, New Zealand, saw an "urgent sale" of a chicken on an online auction site, he thought he was making a bid for just one hen—only to find that his $1.50 actually bought him 1,000 chickens from Auckland farmer Matthew Blomfield. Fortunately, Morrow managed to find homes for the surplus hens.

STORE REUNION

In December 2019, Valerie Sneade and Jason Roy were married at the same Dunkin' Donuts in Worcester, Massachusetts, where they had split up 27 years earlier as youngsters. In the meantime, both had married and divorced.

EYE CANDY CORN

Believe it or not, corn comes in colors other than yellow! Perhaps the most vibrant variety is Glass Gem corn, which can appear in many shades or even a rainbow mixture. But you won't see it on your plate any time soon. Glass Gem is a "flint" corn, meaning the kernel is hard, making it better for cornmeal or popcorn versus being eaten right off the cob. The appropriately named vegetable was first isolated by Oklahoma farmer Carl Barnes, who sought to connect with his Cherokee heritage by growing Native American corn varieties. Barnes died in 2016, but his beautiful produce lives on.

PANCAKE ICE

Rough waters make big pancakes! While most pancakes are concocted with flour, milk, and eggs, the ones shown here are made from waves and air temperatures just below freezing. The water isn't cold enough to freeze completely, so the surface turns into a slush. Moving water causes that thin layer of ice to accumulate into chunks, which collide with each other, smoothing out the sides to create circular pancake ice. These round, frozen flapjacks can measure 1 to 10 ft (0.3 to 3 m) across and up to 4 in (10 cm) thick.

USTRALIAN
LO ART TRAIL

**stralian Silo Art Trail
s more than 4,970 mi
km) and includes
ted silos depicting
ia's story through
ting images.**

st painted silos appeared in
Vestern Australia in 2015, painted
renowned artists, Phlegm and
Brewer), from the UK and the
vely. In the process, they painted
ia's largest outdoor murals to
paintings proved wildly popular,
fusion of masterpieces and trails
tates that collectively make up the
Trail. From 2017 to 2019, rural
alia suffered a severe drought that
pacted small towns and farmers, so
rojects could not have come at a more
me, contributing to renewed hope and

TUMBY BAY SILO ART, SOUTH AUSTRALIA
Artist: Martin Ron
Size: 23,680 sq ft (2,200 sq m)
Paint Used: 114 gal (430 l)
Fun Fact: The artist had to distort the images to compensate
for the curves of the silos, so the mural can only be properly
viewed from a specific point of view.

O ART,
TRALIA
and HENSE
(511 sq m)
gal (740 l)
murals kicked
novement in
artist painted
r signature
is on the left
on the right.

BARRABA SILO ART, NEW SOUTH WALES
Artist: Fintan Magee
Size: 131 ft (40 m) tall
Paint Used: 74 gal (280 l)
Fun Fact: The man featured in the mural is a water diviner. Also known as "dowsing," the practice is hundreds of years old and is supposed to lead the diviner to water hidden underground.

THE GRAINCORP SILOS AT YELARBON, QUEENSLAND
Artist: The Brightsiders
Size: 19,375 sq ft (1,800 sq m)
Paint Used: 740 gal (2,800 l) and 1,500 spray cans
Fun Fact: The artists lived at a Yelarbon pub during the year it took to complete this mural and, in that time, consumed an estimated 283 pints (134 l) of beer!

THE GRAINCORP SILOS AT ROCHESTER, VICTORIA
Artist: Jimmy Dvate
Size: 72 ft (22 m) tall and 49 ft (15 m) tall
Paint Used: 24 gal (90 l) and 116 spray cans
Fun Fact: The species on these silos, the squirrel glider and the azure king fisher, are endemic to Australia, meaning they don't live anywhere else in the world!

THE GRAINCORP SILOS AT SHEEP HILLS, VICTORIA
Artist: Adnate
Size: 12,917 sq ft (1,200 sq m)
Paint Used: 132 gal (500 l) and 250 spray cans
Fun Fact: The mural depicts members of the Barengi Gadjin community, an indigenous group Adnate, the artist, spent three weeks with to develop this design.

NO SPRING CHICKEN

In 1916, one of Sydney's legendary characters, a sulfur-crested Australian cockatoo named Cocky Bennett, passed away at the remarkable age of 120.

Believe it or not, Cocky still holds the record for the longest-lived parrot Down Under. Housed at the Sea Breeze Hotel at Tom Uglys Point in Blakehurst, Cocky delighted guests with his mischievous banter. One of his favorite phrases was "One feather more, and I'll fly!" Despite the cheeky chatter, Cocky Bennett would've had trouble

AVIAN ACCOMMODATIONS

Before the White House's 2020 Turkey Pardoning Ceremony, two lucky gobblers, Corn and Cob, enjoyed a red-carpet rollout and luxurious accommodations at the Willard InterContinental Hotel. This wasn't the first time the four-star hotel opened its doors to feathered friends. In 2014, Tater and Tot spent a night at the luxe establishment, as did Mac and Cheese in 2016. The plush accommodations cost approximately $268 per night, a bill footed by the National Turkey Federation. How does the luxury hotel turkey-proof a room? With plenty of plastic sheeting and pine shavings.

COUGAR DETERRENT

When Dee Gallant spotted a cougar stalking her and her dog while she was hiking in a forest on Vancouver Island, British Columbia, Canada, she scared the big cat away by blasting out Metallica's hit "Don't Tread On Me" on her phone.

BRAIN EATERS

When some species of woodpecker become especially hungry—including the Gila woodpecker of the United States—they will kill smaller birds, pin them down, and peck furiously at the back of their heads until the skull cracks open and the woodpecker is able to eat the brains inside.

CANINE THIEF

When two packages went missing after being left at the front door of the Garza family's home in McAllen, Texas, security camera footage revealed the culprit to be a neighborhood stray dog. On both occasions, the home's doorbell camera showed the dog hanging around waiting patiently for the mailman to leave, then running up to the door, sniffing the package, and stealing it.

TOILET RESCUE

Police officers had to remove a porcelain toilet from a house in Jiangxi Province, China, and smash it in order to rescue a pangolin that was wedged in the back.

SKY MONSTER

A species of flying pterosaur that lived around 200 million years ago had a wingspan of 39 ft (12 m), making it wider than an F-16 fighter jet airplane.

ANT FALL

An ant could fall from the top of the Empire State Building and walk away unharmed. The ant's size and light weight give it a slow terminal velocity, the maximum speed at which something falls through the air. This, combined with the ant's hard exoskeleton, means that even a fall from a great height would not kill or hurt the insect when it hits the ground.

Ripley's Rarities

Ripley's Exhibit
Cat. No. 172646

39-STAR FLAG

Flag makers in 1889 began producing 39-star flags under the assumption that North and South Dakota would be admitted as one state. Instead, they were kept separate, and the country went straight from 38 to 40 states, making the 39-star flag unnecessary.

Ripley's Exhibit
Cat. No. 9233

BAMBOO TOOTHPICK WHITE HOUSE

Designed by Long Hoang of Vietnam and assembled by Linh Vuong and his family in Silver Springs, Maryland, this replica scale model of the White House is made from more than 100,000 bamboo toothpicks. No glue was used; all the pieces are inserted into tiny drilled holes.

Ripley's Exhibit
Cat. No. 173239

LINCOLN BUGLE

Instrument belonging to Hiram Cook, one of President Abraham Lincoln's personal bodyguards. He played this bugle on the night of Lincoln's assassination and again when the President's body was put aboard a train to his home in Illinois.

FAMOUS NAMESAKES

One of the perks of finding a new species is getting to name it. Believe it or not, many scientists choose to name their discoveries after celebrities!

◀ 1 Beyoncé

The unique dense golden hairs found on the abdomen of a rare Australian species of horse fly motivated scientist Bryan Lessard to call it *Scaptia beyonceae* after Beyoncé.

2 Shakira

Colombian singer and belly dancer Shakira inspired the name of a parasitic wasp, *Aleiodes shakirae*, that takes control of its host caterpillar, forcing it to shake and wiggle its abdomen rhythmically.

3 Bob Marley

Paul Sikkel, a field marine biologist at Arkansas University, named a small crustacean parasite after Bob Marley, *Gnathia marleyi*, as a tribute to his music.

4 Darth Vader

Quentin Wheeler, the director of the International Institute for Species Exploration in Arizona, named a slime-mold beetle after Darth Vader (*Agathidium vaderi*) because of its similar-looking eyes and shiny helmet-like head.

5 Kate Winslet

Entomologist Terry Erwin pronounced a beetle *Agra katewinsletae* after Kate Winslet because the insect's endangered plight reminded him of Winslet's harrowing performance in the 1997 movie *Titanic*.

6 David Bowie

German arachnologist Peter Jäger named a particularly vibrant species of spider, *Heteropoda davidbowie*, after the extravagant singer David Bowie, whose discography includes a song titled "Glass Spider."

7 Prince Charles

In recognition of Prince Charles's rainforest charity efforts, scientists named a new species of stream tree frog discovered in Ecuador after him, *Hyloscirtus princecharlesi*.

SHELBY THE BUG GIRL

Cockroaches were just the beginning—she also cares for snakes, butterflies, spiders, and more!

Living with neurofibromatosis—a debilitating genetic disorder that causes tumors to grow on her nerves—has challenged Shelby Counterman, but she draws strength and joy from her collection of more than 5,000 cockroaches.

At just 18 months old, Shelby showed palpable excitement while viewing a tank filled with roaches near her home in Claremore, Oklahoma. Her parents knew what they had to do. Neurofibromatosis made life painful for Shelby. To cheer her up, the Countermans gave her an unusual gift: five Madagascar hissing cockroaches. They proved to be a huge hit. Over the years, Shelby's collection has blossomed to more than 5,000 insects. What does the 13-year-old love most about these misunderstood creatures? The essential role they play in decomposition and cleaning up ecosystems.

Accommodations fit for a king! Shelby's roaches enjoy exploring the castles in their tanks.

Shelby is not afraid to get up close and personal with her pets!

MEMORABLE IMPRESSIONS

Chicago artist Mickey Alice Kwapis specializes in one-of-a-kind mourning jewelry—ash, soil, or hair-filled lockets and vials, plus fingerprint, noseprint, and pawprint molds that she casts into metal charms.

Using a process called "lost wax casting," Kwapis is able to create near-perfect replicas of human or animal prints in a variety of metals, depending on her clients' needs. Other memorabilia, such as hair, ashes, and funeral flowers, may also be incorporated into the finished piece. Kwapis is also a taxidermist, pioneering sustainable techniques in the field and incorporating the practice into her jewelry. As collectors of unusual and rare jewelry and trinkets, Ripley's caught up with Mickey to ask her a few questions about her work.

Artist Mickey Alice Kwapis

Noseprint pendants cast from a dog named Sophie.

Q: How did you end up in the business of taxidermy and mourning jewelry?

A: When I was a kid, I was fascinated by scientific specimens and collecting treasures from nature, so getting involved in taxidermy felt like a natural progression! In college, I started combining elements of taxidermy and nature into my jewelry. When my aunt died, I used preserved flowers from her funeral to make mourning jewelry for the women in my family, and I fell in love with the process of bringing comfort to others through something I made with my hands.

Q: People often avoid thinking about death. What is it like working with this grim reality almost daily?

A: My job is to create sentimental jewelry and other objects for people who have lost a loved one, so it's inevitable that I spend a *lot* of time thinking about life and death. It's beyond devastating to lose a person or animal that you loved and that loved you, so my first concern is always making sure clients take as much time as they need to grieve in a way that feels right for them. Each time I'm chosen to make something like this for someone, I am reminded of what a gift it is that that person had someone they loved so much that they want to hold on to a part of them forever.

A locket filled with all three colors from the coat of a calico cat named Jezebel.

A pendant cast from an actual lion's tooth.

Vial pendants containing—from left to right—a seahorse, scorpion, bee, black widow spider, and diaphonized frog floating in a special liquid, along with gold flakes.

Rings featuring glass eyes used for taxidermy birds.

"My job is to create sentimental jewelry and other objects for people who have lost a loved one, so it's inevitable that I spend a lot of time thinking about life and death."

Q: Which piece is your favorite or has the most meaning to you?

A: The most meaningful piece of jewelry in my own collection is a very small gold locket filled with soil from three different locations on an island called Belle Isle, where my great-grandmother and I spent much of our young lives and time together. When she died at age 102, I found old photos of her in a few of the same spots where I hung out with my friends. I love the idea that mourning jewelry can contain anything you want it to, even beyond actual remains. She passed away on my 30th birthday, and her last gift to me was a Ripley's book from my childhood that fostered my love for all things curious.

SURPRISE VISITOR

In September 2019, high tides from Hurricane Dorian led to a manatee swimming in Corinne Hogan's flooded backyard in St. Lucie County, Florida, where it was seen eating her waterlogged lawn.

CUSTOM SHOES

To cure her foot sores and help her walk more comfortably, Jenny the duck was fitted with a pair of custom orthopedic shoes made from kitchen mats purchased from a local hardware store by Afton, Tennessee, veterinarian Dr. Matt Quillen.

BARE HANDS

A group of men in Costa Rica caught an 8-ft-long (2.4-m) saltwater crocodile—one of the world's deadliest predators—with their bare hands, using just a towel and some string.

DEADLY DISHWASHER

A couple in Paris Creek, South Australia, found a highly venomous eastern brown snake slithering around inside their dishwasher—even though the machine had been running for up to two and a half hours. The snake was believed to have entered via a drainage pipe.

HAWK SNATCH

Deborah Falcione, of Whitehall, Pennsylvania, was reunited with her 16-year-old toy poodle Porschia 28 hours after the dog, who is deaf and blind, was carried off by a hawk. Porschia was snatched from the house's back deck but was dropped by the bird four blocks away, where she was found by a neighbor and taken to a local animal hospital.

SWALLOWED FORK

When Carli Ott shared a piece of pumpkin pie with Chemo, her four-year-old bullmastiff boxer mix, the dog also swallowed the metal fork Ott was holding. Veterinarians in Cleveland, Texas, performed surgery to remove the fork from the dog's digestive system.

CANINE FUGITIVE

Payton, a female mixed breed dog that escaped from a rescue center near Columbus, Ohio, was finally captured two months later after traveling around 65 mi (104 km) and being spotted 22 times.

RAT DRIVERS

Scientists at the University of Richmond, Virginia, trained rats to drive tiny cars to reach food.

SERVICE HORSE

In February 2020, Ronica Froese, from Croton, Michigan, took her miniature support horse Fred on several American Airlines flights from Grand Rapids, Michigan, to Ontario, California. The pair traveled first class, and Fred wore a superhero costume bearing the words "Service Horse."

BAT INVASION

In December 2019, 1,700 bats invaded a small balcony on an apartment building in Lviv, Ukraine, and occupied corners, cupboards, and drawers as they looked for a warm spot where they could mate.

FLOCK TOGETHER

It turns out sheepdogs can herd more than just sheep! Pip and Tilly, two border collie rescues, help farmer Steve Childerhouse move 10,000 turkeys from place to place at Whews Farm in Norfolk, England. Childerhouse says it took a little time for both the dogs and turkeys to get used to the arrangement, but once they did, it made his job much easier.

SLIM PICKINGS

Actual size of a baby sunfish!

Ocean sunfish transform from pinhead-sized, spike-covered babies into the world's largest bony fish, measuring upward of 14 × 10 ft (4.2 × 3 m) and weighing up to 5,000 lb (2,268 kg)!

Growth-curve estimates of captive individuals suggest a lifespan of more than two decades, but scientists have been unable to confirm this. These underwater flying saucers swim by flapping their "wings" and steering their pseudo-tail. Because of their dinner plate–like shape, ocean sunfish (*Mola molas*) are a tempting treat to more than 50 species of parasites. How do the fish cope? By floating to the ocean's surface, where albatross, gulls, and other seabirds rip the nasty critters out of their flesh.

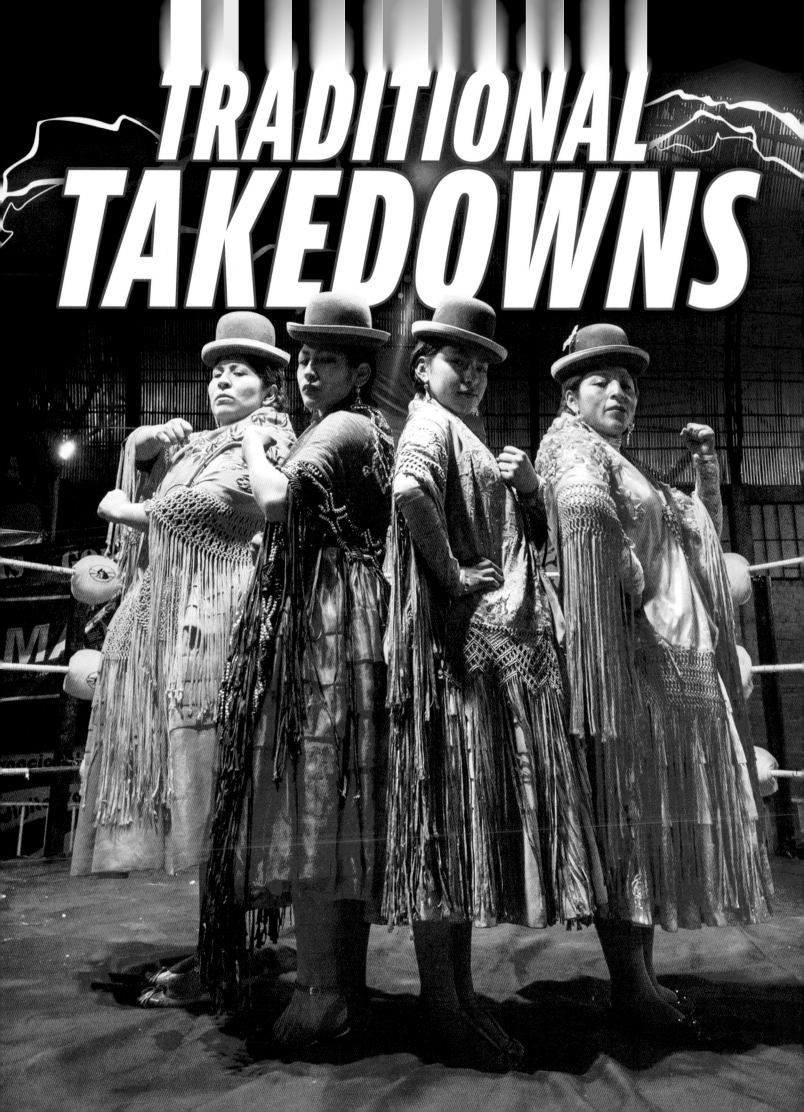

TRADITIONAL TAKEDOWNS

Dressed in traditional clothing, indigenous women in Bolivia enter the wrestling ring not just to fight each other but also to battle against harmful stereotypes.

Known as "cholitas," a once-derogatory term that has been reclaimed, Aymara and Quechua women blend the theatrics of the WWE with traditional aspects of Mexican lucha libre. Wearing layered skirts, sandals, pigtail braids, and bowler hats, cholitas perform in front of hundreds of spectators, tossing each other around with perfectly practiced maneuvers. And while the fights may be "fake," the moves are real and require intensive training.

Cholita wrestling is about 20 years young, but it has made an impact nonetheless. These strong women defy gender stereotypes, teach techniques in self-defense, and are also vocal advocates for political movements. Through wrestling, they make their communities safer and stronger.

THE ADVENTURE BEGINS HERE!

There are more than 100 fun-filled Ripley's Attractions worldwide!

From our classic Believe It or Not! Odditoriums to our world-class Aquariums, you can find what's closest to you at Ripleys.com.

RIPLEY'S SUPER FUN ZONE

RIPLEY'S HAUNTED ADVENTURE

RIPLEY'S RED TRAIN TOURS

RIPLEY'S AQUARIUMS

ACKNOWLEDGMENTS

4 (l) Courtesy of Erin Blaire and DeAndre Bennett, (tr) Courtesy of Caroline Eriksson, (br) Simon J Pierce - www.simonjpierce.com **5** (t) Georgia Tech Photo: Rob Felt, (bl) Ernie Ostuno, (br) © Kertu/Shutterstock.com **10–11** (bkg) © Titima Ongkantong/Shutterstock.com **11** (tr) walpaperlist.com, (cl) © Filipchuk Maksym/Shutterstock.com **12–13** (bkg) REUTERS/Kathleen Flynn/Alamy Stock Photo **13** (t, c, b) © Suzanne C. Grim/Shutterstock.com **14** © reptiles4all/Shutterstock.com **15** Paul Bertner/Minden Pictures **16** (t) Claire Hogan/Caters News, (b) Kendra Williams **17** (tl, tr) Roger Hutchings/Alamy Stock Photo, (b) london road via flickr (CC BY 2.0) **18–21** (bkg) Ocean Alliance/Christian Miller **22–23** (t) Courtesy of Ran, IG @konel_bread **23** (b) Courtesy of Peter J. Wilt **24** (t) Christopher Dens/CATERS NEWS, (b) Courtesy of Nathan Cabrera **25** SWNS **28** (tl) © Globe Photos/ZUMA Wire/Alamy Stock Photo, (b) Picture Perfect/Shutterstock **29** (tl) Sony/Shutterstock, (tr) Abc-Tv/Kobal/Shutterstock, (b) © Kathy Hutchins/Shutterstock.com **30–31** (t) Anastasia Andreeva/Asya Kozina/Dmitriy Kozin/Cover Images **30** (br) © Africa Studio/Shutterstock.com **32** (tl) © KarenHBlack/Shutterstock.com, (tr) © Jedsada Naeprai/Shutterstock.com, (cl) © Elzbieta Sekowska/Shutterstock.com, (cr) © Erni/Shutterstock.com, (b) © Jordi C/Shutterstock.com **33** (t) Nature Picture Library/Alamy Stock Photo, (b) Xinhua/Liu Xiao via Getty Images **34** Courtesy of Ben Jacoby and Ofer Yakov **35** Courtesy of Colin Thomas Darke **36** Lorie Shaull via flickr (CC BY-SA 2.0) **37** (t) MANDEL NGAN/AFP via Getty Images, (cl) Glessner House, (b) Lorie Shaull via flickr (CC BY-SA 2.0) **38** (t) SWNS, (b) © Dmitriy Efremychev/Shutterstock.com **39** (t) Mark Andrews/Alamy Stock Photo, (b) Xinhua/Alamy Stock Photo **40–41** KEN BUTLER/CATERS NEWS **42** Courtesy of Chas Moonie **43** Steve Lonhart via (SIMoN/MBNMS) U.S. National Oceanic and Atmospheric Administration (Public Domain) **44** Courtesy of Amadeus López **45** Courtesy of Erin Blaire and DeAndre Bennett **46–47** (bkg) © R.M. Nunes/Shutterstock.com **46** (t) © Guitar photographer/Shutterstock.com, (b) © steph photographies/Shutterstock.com **47** (tr) © Olga Vasilyeva/Shutterstock.com **48** Tracey Smith/MERCURY PRESS/CATERS NEWS **49** (t) Ingo Arndt/Nature Picture Library, (b) Dr Farvardin Daliri www.favardindaliri.com **52** STR/AFP via Getty Images **53** SWNS **54–55** Camilo Freedman/APHOTOGRAFIA/Getty Images **55** (bl) ElmerGuevara via Wikimedia (CC BY-SA 3.0) **56** (tl) © Peter Hermes Furian/Shutterstock.com, (cl) © Andrey_Kuzmin/Shutterstock.com, (cr) © oksana2010/Shutterstock.com, (br) © Africa Studio/Shutterstock.com **57** Courtesy of Caroline Eriksson **58** (t) © Fabio Ara/Shutterstock.com, (b) Antony van der Ent, The University of Queensland, Australia. **59** © ChinKC/Shutterstock.com **60–61** (t) Lexus UK **60** (b) © Ungvari Attila/Shutterstock.com **62–63** Matthew Van Vorst, @cuttin_the_cheese **63** (bl, bc) @cuttin_the_cheese/Caters News **64** (t) James Owen Thomas/Caters News, (b) © Christos Georghiou/Shutterstock.com **65** Delicious Mr Darcy commissioned for TV channel Drama on UKTV Play **66** Instagram @vasilisafreestyle.1 **67** Courtesy of Dan Wasdahl and Joseph Albert **70** (t) REUTERS/Alamy Stock Photo, (b, br) Chris Humphrey/dpa/Alamy Live News **71** The Brick Wall/Cover Images **72** (tl) © mamboo/Shutterstock.com, (tr) © VladimirSVK/Shutterstock.com, (cl) © Trudy Wilkerson/Shutterstock.com, (cr) © Karel Bartik/Shutterstock.com, (b) © Jay Ondreicka/Shutterstock.com **73** (bkg) © volkova natalia/Shutterstock.com, (cr) © Seregraff/Shutterstock.com **74–75** © Christin Marinoni **75** (t) Courtesy of Clay Mazing **76** Courtesy of Clay Mazing **77** (t, b) © Christin Marinoni, (c) Courtesy of Clay Mazing **78** © SewCream/Shutterstock.com **79** Photononstop/Alamy Stock Photo **80** (t) Zhang Weiguo/VCG via Getty Images, (b) Photo taken by Kelly Rigoni **81** Satoshi Nagare/The Nippon Foundation/Cover Images **82–83** Ivan Djuric/Caters News **82** (tr) © Olga Moonlight/Shutterstock.com **84** (t) Earth Science and Remote Sensing Unit, NASA Johnson Space Center (Public Domain), (b) tony_rodd via flickr (CC BY-NC-SA 2.0) **85** (bkg) JEFFREY GROENEWEG/ANP/AFP via Getty Images, (br) REUTERS/Eva Plevier/Alamy Stock Photo **86–91** (bkg) © Andrey_Kuzmin/Shutterstock.com **86, 89** (t) © rangizzz/Shutterstock.com **92** (t) Wellcome Collection (CC BY 4.0), (c) Daily Herald Archive/SSPL/Getty Images, (b) J. Willis Sayre Collection of Theatrical Photographs from University of Washington: Special Collections via Wikimedia Commons (Public Domain) **93** (t) © Ruslan Lytvyn/Shutterstock.com, (c) © Vasyl Rohan/Shutterstock.com, (b) © Oleksandr Berezko/Shutterstock.com **94–95** Tarso Marques/Cover Images **94** (bl, br) Renani Jewels/Cover Images **96** (t) STEVE HATHAWAY/CATERS NEWS, (b) Nature Picture Library/Alamy Stock Photo **97** Chase Dekker/Minden Pictures **100** (t) The Courier-Journal via Wikimedia Commons (Public Domain), (c) dbking via flickr(CC BY 2.0), (br) Polish Press Agency (PAP) via Wikimedia Commons (Public Domain) **101** (t) CBS Photo Archive/Getty Images, (bkg) © mark reinstein/Shutterstock.com, (b) Frank Augstein/AP/Shutterstock **102** Beth M. Bays **103** Luis Nostromo/Cover Images **104** (tl) Hubert Duprat via Wikimedia (CC BY-SA 3.0), (tr) Avalon.red/Alamy Stock Photo, (b) © davemhuntphotography/Shutterstock.com **105** Paul Christian Gordon/Alamy Stock Photo **106** (t) REUTERS/Alamy Stock Photo, (b) Courtesy of Uruguay Minerals **107** Love Hulten **108–111** www.fionaparkinson.com Instagram – @fiona_taxidermy **112** (tl) Adams Wood/Barcroft Media/Barcroft Media via Getty Images, (tr) Jason Blalock/Barcroft Media via Getty Images, (bl) LocoWiki via Wikimedia (CC BY-SA 4.0), (bc) Rabia S Ahmad via Wikimedia (CC BY 4.0), (br) Courtesy of Elaine Kicknosway **113** Istvan Lettang/Barcroft Media via Getty Images **114–115** (t) dbking via flickr (CC BY 2.0) **115** (tr) FBI (Public Domain), (tl) George Skadding/The LIFE Picture Collection via Getty Images, (bl, br) Caters News/Sonia Barton **118** Noah Sheidlower **119** SWNS **120–121** Simon J Pierce at naturetripper.com **122** (t) Subhankar Chakraborty/Hindustan Times via Getty Images, (b) Qu Honglun/China News Service/Visual China Group via Getty Images **123** Uwe Zucchi/picture alliance via Getty Images **124** (b) Biblio Photography/Alamy Stock Photo, (cl) © Steely Images/Shutterstock.com **125** Bonhams/BNPS **126** (tl) SWNS, (cr) SWNS **126–127** (bkg) Jhony Islas/AP/Shutterstock **127** (tr) © videobuzzing/Shutterstock.com, (cr) © Daniel Prudek/Shutterstock.com **128** (tl) Anton Sorokin/Alamy Stock Photo, (tr) © Awei/Shutterstock.com, (bl) © Ryan M. Bolton/Shutterstock.com, (br) BIOSPHOTO/Alamy Stock Photo **129** Paul Bertner/Minden Pictures **130** (t) Kelvin Aitken/VWPics/Alamy Stock Photo, (br) Ocean Exploration Trust via marinespecies.org (CC BY-NC-SA 4.0), (bl) © SergioRocha/Shutterstock.com **131** (t) ARFA/AFP via Getty Images, (b) Basri Marzuki/NurPhoto via Getty Images **134** (t) © Luca Lorenzelli/Shutterstock.com, (cl) Photogilio/Alamy Stock Photo **135** (bkg, br) Imaginechina Limited/Alamy Stock Photo, (cl) © OLOS/Shutterstock.com **136** Nature Picture Library/Alamy Stock Photo **137** (tl, tr, cr) SWNS, (bl, br) AURORA RUTLEDGE/CATERS NEWS **138–139** Ian Berry/Cover Images **138** (bl) Debbie Bragg/Cover Images **139** (c) Debbie Bragg/Cover Images **140** (t) Bettmann/Contributor, (bl) © Alvydas Kucas/Shutterstock.com, (b) © Jacob_09/Shutterstock.com **141** Courtesy of Hasan Kaval **142** (t) © cowardlion/Shutterstock.com, (b) robertharding/Alamy Stock Photo **143** (t) © Shawn.ccf/Shutterstock.com, (b) © Perati Komson/Shutterstock.com **144** Courtesy of Menga **144–145** © Mikhail Priakhin/Shutterstock.com **145** © Mikhail Priakhin/Shutterstock.com **146** (t) © Bryan Millar Walker/Shutterstock.com, (cr) JOHN BRACEGIRDLE/Alamy Stock Photo **147** Marit Hommedal/EPA-EFE/Shutterstock **148** (t) © ForceAlex/Shutterstock.com, (c) © KUCO/Shutterstock.com, (b) © Foto-Ruhrgebiet/Shutterstock.com **149** (t, cr) Ernie Ostuno, (b) TPG/Getty Images **150** (t, b) © Hethers/Shutterstock.com, (bl) © CK Travels/Shutterstock.com **151** (tl, t) Architect of the Capitol via flickr (Public Domain), (b) Richard Huber (CC BY-SA 4.0) **152** (t) Courtesy of Brianna Vorhees, (b, br) DEBBIE WALLACE/CATERS NEWS **153** @jazzy.purrs - Instagram **156** Imaginechina Limited/Alamy Stock Photo **157** (t) Yomiuri Shimbun via AP Images, (bl) The Asahi Shimbun/Getty Images **158–159** (t) Leopold Nekula/Sygma via Getty Images **158** (bl) volkerpreusser/Alamy Stock Photo **159** (bl) Claus Felix/picture alliance via Getty Images, (cr) MediaWorldImages/Alamy Stock Photo **160** (t) Dilantha Dissanayake/CATERS NEWS, (bl, br) Kristina Dolnyk/Cover Images **161** Magnus Lundgren/naturepl.com **162** Wang Qingqin/Xinhua/Sipa/Shutterstock **163** (tl) Derek Beeman/Jenna Beeman, (b) © Delmas Lehman/Shutterstock.com **164** (bl) Lucas Vallecillos/VWPics/Alamy Stock Photo **164–165** (t) mauritius images GmbH/Alamy Stock Photo, (b) Agencja Fotograficzna Caro/Alamy Stock Photo **165** (cr) © travelarium.ph/Shutterstock.com **166** Bill and Ted's Excellent Adventure characters and images ™ & © 1989, 2021 Creative Licensing Corporation. All Rights Reserved **167** Courtesy of Linda Verhoeff and Henk Verhoeff **168** (t) GG Conservation/Caters News, (b) Courtesy of Christine Watts **169** (bkg) agefotostock/Alamy Stock Photo, (bl) © Smiler99/Shutterstock.com **170** (tl) © ackats/Shutterstock.com, (cl) Eckhard Pecher via Wikimedia (CC BY 2.5), (cr) © 22Images Studio/Shutterstock.com, (b) © Anthony McLaughlin/Shutterstock.com **171** (t, tr) Courtesy of Jessica Zhang, (cl, cr, bl, br) © Travers Lewis/Shutterstock.com **174** (tl) © Jeff Bukowski/Shutterstock.com, (tr) The Susan Jaffe Tane Collection, Cornell University via Wikimedia Commons (Public Domain), (bl) British Library via Wikimedia Commons (Public Domain) **175** (tl) Harris Brisbane Dick Fund, 1924 via Metropolitan Museum of Art (CC0 1.0), (tr) Unknown author; Restored by Yann Forget and Adam Cuerden via Wikimedia Commons (Public Domain), (br) KRichter via Wikimedia Commons (Public Domain) **176** Jorge Saenz/AP/Shutterstock **176–177** Facebook: Bartz Snow Sculptures **178–179** REUTERS/Nacho Doce/Alamy Stock Photo **180** Kyle Marquart, @Kyle_and_Pyro **181** (bkg) © Olivier Guiberteau/Shutterstock.com, (bl) Zip Lexing/Alamy Stock Photo **182–183** (t) Mustafa Ozturk/Anadolu Agency via Getty Images **183** (tc) Mustafa Ozturk/Anadolu Agency via Getty Images, (bl, br) SWNS **184** (t) Alex & Rebecca May, (b) Dave Watts/Alamy Stock Photo **185** Tony Wu/naturepl.com **186** (tl) PA Images/Alamy Stock Photo, (cl) © Silvia Elizabeth Pangaro/Shutterstock.com, (cr) © encierro/Shutterstock.com, (bl) Francis Specker/Alamy Stock Photo **187** (tr, c) SWNS, (br) Airbnb/Cover Images **188–189** George Rose/Getty Images **190** Hatem Moussa/AP/Shutterstock **191** Imaginechina Limited/Alamy Stock Photo **194** (l) Jules Chéret via Wikimedia Commons (Public Domain), (r) © benchart/Shutterstock.com, (rc) The John R. Van Derlip Fund via The Minneapolis Institute of Art (Public Domain) **195** (l) © benchart/Shutterstock.com, (lc) The John R. Van Derlip Fund via The Minneapolis Institute of Art (Public Domain), (tr) Jules Cheret/Alamy Stock Photo, (cr) UPI/Alamy Stock Photo, (b) Northwest Museum of Arts & Culture/Eastern Washington State Historical Society, Gift of Jeanne Keck and Barbara Oehler, 1981, 2790.7 **196** (tr) Sergi Reboredo/Alamy Stock Photo, (bkg) Hemis/Alamy Stock Photo, (bl) Westend61 GmbH/Alamy Stock Photo **197** Ariana Cubillos/AP/Shutterstock **198** (t) Stephen Zozaya via Wikimedia Commons (CC BY 2.5), (b) Elaventhan/CATERS NEWS **199** (bkg) Magnus Lundgren/NPL/Minden Pictures, (br) © Leonardo Gonzalez/Shutterstock.com **200–201** (bkg) © Sing Studio/Shutterstock.com **200** (t) © DerekTeo/Shutterstock.com, (b) Ore Huiying/Getty Images **202** CHINE NOUVELLE/SIPA/Shutterstock **203** Costfoto/Barcroft Media via Getty Images **204** (t) Jean Chung/Getty Images, (b, cr) David Guralnick/The Detroit News/TNS/Tribune Content Agency LLC/Alamy Stock Photo **205** (bkg) AFP via Getty Images, (b) © Hulton-Deutsch Collection/CORBIS/Corbis via Getty Images **206** Steven D. Emslie **207** (t) Smith Archive/Alamy Stock Photo, (b) Alan D. Wilson via Nature's Pics Online (CC BY-SA 3.0) **208** (tl) Elliott & Fry via Wikimedia Commons (Public Domain), (cl) Frank Powolny via Wikimedia Commons (Public Domain), (cr) NASA (Public Domain), (bl) Napoleon Sarony LC-DIG-ppmsca-07757 via Library of Congress (Public Domain) **209** Courtesy of Fashion Brand Company and Penelope Gazin **210–211** Lumilor India **212** ARCTIC IMAGES/Alamy Stock Photo **213** (t) © klublu/Shutterstock.com, (cl) JAIME REINA/AFP via Getty Images, (b) PA Images/Alamy Stock Photo **214** (t) Getty Images for EIF & XQ, (b) Courtesy of Nicoletta Bates **215** (tl, bl) Steven Van Aerschot/Alamy Stock Photo, (tr, br) Imaginechina Limited/Alamy Stock Photo **218** (t) Frank Glaw/SNSB/ZSM/Cover Images, (b) David Shale/naturepl.com **219** (t) Nature's Images/Science Source, (b) © Andrea Florence/ardea.com **220–221** © Joe Nafis/Shutterstock.com **220** REUTERS/Alamy Stock Photo **222** (bkg) Roland Seitre/Minden Pictures, (tl) © Diana Taliun/Shutterstock.com, (br) © Susan Flashman/Shutterstock.com **223** (t) Georgia Tech Photo: Rob Felt, (br) © Eric Isselee/Shutterstock.com **224** REUTERS/Alamy Stock Photo **225** (t, c) REUTERS/Alamy Stock Photo, (b) JC20940 via Wikimedia Commons (CC BY-SA 4.0) **226** (tl, tr) Caters News, (bl) © Leigh Prather/Shutterstock.com **227** SWNS **228–229** (bkg) © Kertu/Shutterstock.com **228** © Alexey Vymyatnin/Shutterstock.com **229** (t) © Kertu/Shutterstock.com, (c) © Vlad Sokolovsky/Shutterstock.com, (b) © Riska Parakeet/Shutterstock.com **230** Photo credit: Megan Ayers, Instagram: meg.ayers **231** (t) © ThomasLENNE/Shutterstock.com, (b) Gary Cook/Alamy Stock Photo **232–233** (bkg) © mainfu/Shutterstock.com **232** (tr) Courtesy of Martin Ron and Annette Green, (bl, br) Art by Phlegm and Hense, photograph by Bewley Shaylor, images courtesy of FORM **233** (tl) Courtesy of Fintan Magee, (tr) Courtesy of The Brightsiders and Jordache Castilllejos, (cr) Courtesy of Jimmy Dvate and Annette Green, (br) Courtesy of Adnate **234** Courtesy of the Local Studies Collection, Sutherland Shire Libraries (Public Domain) **235** Cover Images **238** (tl) © Featureflash Photo Agency/Shutterstock.com, (tr) Bryan D. Lessard/CSIRO via scienceimage.csiro.au (CC BY 3.0), (cr) Seshadri.K.S via Wikimedia Commons (CC BY-SA 4.0), (b) Arcasapos via Wikimedia Commons (GNU FDL) **239** (bkg) © DayNightArt/Shutterstock.com, (tl, bl, br) Meg Counterman **240–241** Mickey Alice Kwapis **242** CATERS NEWS **243** (bkg) Daniel Botelho/Barcroft Media via Getty Images, (br) Courtesy of Matt Wittenrich and Dr. Jon Shenker of Florida Institute of Technology. **244–245** (t) © HaseHoch2/Shutterstock.com, © sunsinger/Shutterstock.com **Master graphics** Luis Fuentes, © Filipchuk Maksym/Shutterstock.com, © Vasya Kobelev/Shutterstock.com, © Titima Ongkantong/Shutterstock.com © wenani/Shutterstock.com

Key: t = top, b = bottom, c = center, l = left, r = right, bkg = background

All other photos are from Ripley Entertainment, Inc. Every attempt has been made to acknowledge correctly and contact copyright holders and we apologize in advance for any unintentional errors or omissions, which will be corrected in future editions.

Connect with Ripley's Online or in Person

28
EXTRAORDINARY LOCATIONS

There are 28 incredible Ripley's Believe It or Not! Odditoriums all around the world, where you can experience our spectacular collection!

Amsterdam THE NETHERLANDS
Atlantic City NEW JERSEY
Blackpool ENGLAND
Branson MISSOURI
Cavendish P.E.I., CANADA
Copenhagen DENMARK
Dubai UNITED ARAB EMIRATES
Gatlinburg TENNESSEE
Genting Highlands MALAYSIA
Grand Prairie TEXAS
Guadalajara MEXICO
Hollywood CALIFORNIA
Mexico City MEXICO
Myrtle Beach SOUTH CAROLINA
New York City NEW YORK
Newport OREGON
Niagara Falls ONTARIO, CANADA
Ocean City MARYLAND
Orlando FLORIDA
Panama City Beach FLORIDA
Pattaya THAILAND
San Antonio TEXAS
San Francisco CALIFORNIA
St. Augustine FLORIDA
Surfers Paradise AUSTRALIA
Veracruz MEXICO
Williamsburg VIRGINIA
Wisconsin Dells WISCONSIN

Stop by our website daily for new stories, photos, contests, and more! **www.ripleys.com**
Don't forget to connect with us on social media for a daily dose of the weird and the wonderful.

/RipleysBelieveItOrNot
@Ripleys
youtube.com/Ripleys
@RipleysBelieveItorNot
@RipleysBelieveItorNot
@ripleysbelieveitornot

Peeing on a jellyfish sting does not stop the pain. In fact, it may actually cause the sea creature's nematocysts to inject even more venom into its victim! So, what should you do if you get stung by a jellyfish? Experts recommend treating it by immediately washing the skin in vinegar to stop the nematocysts from discharging more venom. Rinsing the sting in freshwater will actually intensify the pain because it disturbs the balance of salts in the stingers.

The Great Wall of China is big, but not big enough to be seen from space. Believe it or not, both American and Chinese astronauts have confirmed that neither the Moon nor the International Space Station offer a view of the Great Wall. Alan Bean, of the *Apollo 12* mission, recounts that all you can really make out on the Earth are lots of white clouds and snow, some blue patches, a little bit of yellow, and—every once in a while—a patch of green.

While it likely wouldn't hurt to drink more water, you're probably doing better than you think. The classic advice to drink eight 8-ounce glasses of water each day, which has been emblazened on posters hanging in grade school gyms for decades, may be a bit of overkill. While it is true that around 2,000 milliliters of water each day are recommended to go along with a standard diet, the water doesn't have to be in its purest form—fruit and many other foods, plus almost every beverage, contain some form of water that count toward that recommended amount.

263

A black belt does not equal mastery in martial arts. This achievement simply means the learner has mastered all of the basic defense maneuvers—blocks, kicks, and punches. Black belt, "shodan" in Japanese, translates to "first step." More knowledge can always be added to a practitioner's repertoire, which is why there are first-degree, second-degree, third-degree, and so on classifications of the black belt.

Touching a baby bird will not make the mother abandon it. The cautionary belief that a mother bird will smell a human scent on her nestling and desert it is commonly told to children to keep them from disturbing small animals. The truth is, most birds don't have a great sense of smell! They're also fiercely protective of their babies and not likely to leave them on their own too early. However, this doesn't mean it's okay to disturb the wildlife. If you see a baby bird on its own, it is probably just learning to fly and its mother isn't far away.

Napoleon Bonaparte wasn't particularly short. His nickname, "le petit caporal," was really just a term of endearment rather than a jab at his height, but his enemies used it against him. To perpetuate the rumor that he was short, both before and after his death, other countries created slanderous propaganda. At the time of his death, his height might have been recorded in French inches, which were a little longer than English inches. He was put at 5 feet 2 inches (1.57 meters), but this was probably more like 5 feet 6.5 inches (1.69 meters), a perfectly normal height for a man of his time.

That piece of gum you swallowed three years ago? It's long gone. Despite the oft-repeated wisdom on the schoolyard playground, it doesn't take seven years to digest swallowed gum. Your body won't be able to break the gum base (made out of synthetic and natural polymers) down in seven years, but that does not mean it won't be able to expel the gum from your body. Instead of just sitting in your stomach, a regular piece of swallowed gum will move through your small intestine to your colon and then pass as regular waste when you go to the bathroom.

Opossums don't actually play dead when they're threatened.
Instead, they involuntarily enter a catatonic state. When threatened, it will drop to the ground and close its eyes or stare off into space. Its body goes limp, its breathing appears to stop, it discharges its bowels, its tongue sticks out, and it drools. If you poke it, the opossum will not respond. By all indications, it appears to be dead. The animal doesn't feel any pain and has no reflexes when this occurs. It even stops blinking its eyes. An opossum won't respond no matter what a predator does, even if swats, bites, or breaks the opossum's bones!

That red juice oozing out of your steak is not blood! By the time meat reaches your local grocery store, most of the blood has been removed from the muscle. The red color you are seeing is actually caused by a protein called myoglobin, which is found in muscle tissue and contains a red pigment. Cow muscle has more myoglobin than chicken, pig, or sheep muscle does, which is partially why the meat is a different color—not because it contains more blood.

Goldfish can live for a surprisingly long time. Take a beat the next time you think about trying to win a goldfish at the state fair, as it might not be the short-term commitment you're imagining. When properly cared for, most pet goldfish can live for at least a decade. Incredibly, some goldfish have been known to reach their forties!

A camel's hump does not contain water. Camels can drink as much as 32 gallons (121 liters) of water in 15 minutes, but it is not stored in the humps! The humps are used to store fat, which enables them to go days without food when traversing the desert. Camels can survive a week without drinking water and several months without eating.

Different parts of the tongue do not taste different flavors.
You may be familiar with a colorful diagram of the tongue
from your elementary school classroom that clearly labeled
specialized regions for different flavor profiles. But in reality,
all regions of the tongue capable of tasting can identify all five
qualities—sweet, sour, salty, bitter, and umami (savory).

Concrete shoes aren't an effective means of murder. If you've ever watched a mobster movie, you've probably heard the phrase "sleeping with the fishes" paired with ominous music. This phrase means that the mafia had weighed down a victim with concrete and disposed of them in a body of water. In reality, however, it takes hours for concrete to harden. So while very dramatic, it isn't the quickest way to get rid of a body, making it a rare form of mobster murder.

A dog's mouth is not cleaner than a human's. While a human's mouth is a veritable cesspool of microorganisms, a dog spends its day sticking its tongue into all sorts of questionable places. Some rumors have even been floated that dog saliva can ward off infection, but dog saliva is just as dirty as human saliva. The idea that it is "cleaner" stems from the fact that dogs have different types of bacteria present in their mouths and when doing a one-to-one comparison, have less of the specific types of bacteria that humans do.

Fortune cookies are not originally Chinese. The concept for the tiny after-dinner desserts actually started in Japan as bigger, darker-colored fortune cookies with messages inside their creases. These *senbei*, or "crackers" were invented in the late 19th century—if not earlier—and are still being made in Japan today. They made their way to San Francisco and Los Angeles, California, in the early 1900s, where local Chinese restaurants began including them on their menus.

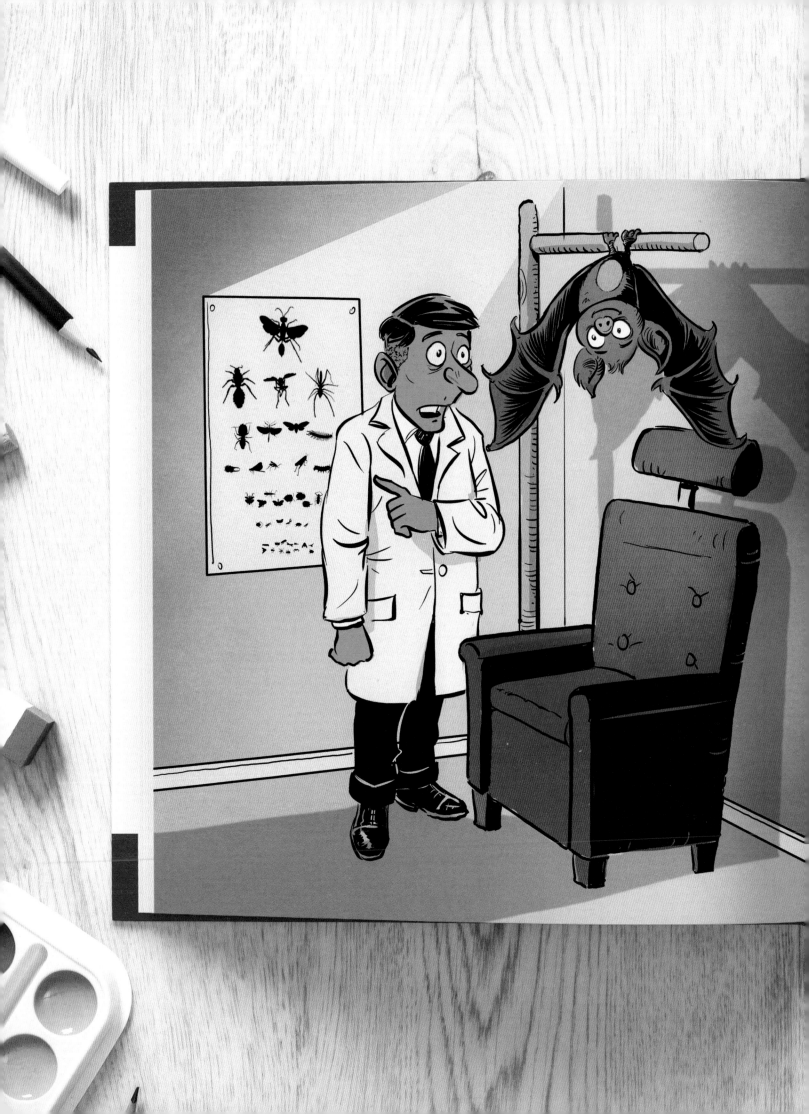

Bats aren't really "blind as a bat." In fact, some bats can see three times better than humans! Many bats can also see ultraviolet light, which is a wavelength of color that people can't even detect. Bats are known for using echolocation. They navigate the world using echoes, which bounce off of objects and help them pinpoint a location. This behavior has boosted the myth that bats only use sound to get around.

You don't actually swallow spiders during your sleep! The urban legend has varied throughout the years, with some proclaiming the average person eats about eight spiders a year while sleeping, but you can rest assured (literally) knowing that spiders will not willingly approach a sleeping person's mouth. Spiders can sense vibrations—humans put off all kinds of them while in dreamland—and will avoid them when possible. What's more, you are likely to wake up if you feel something moving across your face!

Snake don't dislocate their jaws! Unlike mammals, the mandibles—lower jawbones—of snakes remain unfused. Instead, stretchy ligaments bind these moveable pieces of a snake's jaw in place—until it's time to dive into a big meal. Loosely joined at the back of the skull, their mandibles permit greater rotation than most animals. As a result, snakes can open their mouths wider than their bodies. Plus, the two lower jaws move independently of one another, giving the appearance of dislocation.

Marie Antoinette never said the phrase, "Let them eat cake." Instead, it came from a book published in 1782 titled *Confessions* by Jean-Jacques Rousseau. It came out 11 years before Marie Antoinette was executed, but became incredibly popular during the Revolution. Believe it or not, the line was actually written as, "Let them eat brioche." Folklore experts have also found a similar phrase used in German stories from the 1600s, only this time cake and brioche are replaced with *krosem*—German sweet bread.

Real ninjas didn't dress in all black. While Hollywood has done an excellent job of filling our heads with the iconic image of black-clad, sword-wielding ninjas, this couldn't be further from the truth. The function and mission of each ninja was different, not unlike contemporary CIA agents, and they would assume the image of an inconspicuous member of society. The deadliest weapon a ninja could possess? Blending in!

The "fact" that sharks can detect a drop of blood from a mile away is exaggerated. Some sharks can identify blood a quarter-mile away, but the scent doesn't reach them instantaneously or necessarily cause them to attack. Smells reach a shark through the currents, and it would take time for the scent to travel that distance to a shark's nostrils. If you do start to bleed while swimming in the ocean, there is some time to get safely to shore in case a rogue shark decides to attack.

Eating extra carrots does not improve your vision. Most eye issues are caused by genetics, aging, or diabetes, and a carrot's beta carotene properties won't fix your vision, just help maintain it. The myth of carrots improving your eyesight came about during World War II, when the British government credited carrots for helping their Air Force see better while hunting down German aircraft at night.

Touching a toad or one peeing on you will not give you warts. There are many different types of warts, but none of them are caused by toads or frogs. They are instead caused by the human papillomavirus (or HPV), which can result in the multiplication of cells on the outside of your skin, creating a bump. Warts aren't dangerous, treating them usually isn't a problem, and in no way are they caused by amphibians.

SHOP THE STRANGE

Show off your love of the strange and unusual with everything from apparel to books, accessories, mugs, and more!